Changemakers

Changemakers

*How Leaders Can Design Change
in an Insanely Complex World*

**Maria Giudice
Christopher Ireland**

TWO WAVES
BOOKS

NEW YORK, NY, USA

Changemakers

How Leaders Can Design Change in an Insanely Complex World

by Maria Giudice and Christopher Ireland

Design & Production

Publisher: Louis Rosenfeld
Managing Editor: Marta Justak
Illustrations & Diagrams: Aino Horsma
Interior Design: MINE™
Interior Layout Tech: David Van Ness
Cover Design: The Heads of State
Indexer: Marilyn Augst
Proofreader: Chuck Hutchinson

Typography

Text: Lyon Text *from* Commercial Type
Display: Brenner Slab *from* Typotheque
Sans Serif: Graphik *from* Commercial Type

Two Waves Books

an Imprint of Rosenfeld Media
125 Maiden Lane
New York, New York
USA

Online: twowavesbooks.com
Errors: errata@twowavesbooks.com

Paperback ISBN: 1-959029-14-2
ISBN-13: 978-1-959029-14-4
LCCN: 2022943939

Printed and bound in the USA

To my mother, Carol Frazzetta,
*a changemaker and role model who broke through
barriers to design a life worth living*

— Maria Giudice

To Davis,
who changed everything

— Christopher Ireland

Contents

viii   **Contributors**

Kat Holmes
x   **Foreword**

Chapter 1
1   **The Imperfect Future**

Chapter 2
21   **Becoming a Changemaker**

Chapter 3
35   **Finding a Fit**

Chapter 4
51   **Foundations of Success**

Chapter 5
65   **Co-Creating Change**

Chapter 6
81   **Following a Map**

Chapter 7

101 **Shaping the Narrative**

Chapter 8

119 **Building Support**

Chapter 9

139 **Discover What's Possible**

Chapter 10

161 **Envisioning the Outcome**

Chapter 11

181 **Learning What Works**

Chapter 12

197 **When Things Go Wrong**

Chapter 13

215 **When Things Go Right**

Chapter 14

229 **Evolving by Design**

246 **Index**

256 **Acknowledgments**

258 **About the Authors**

Contributors

Lauralee Alben
Founder & CEO,
Sea Change Design Institute

Sunny Bates
Founder, redthread.is
Co-founder of Sudden Compass

Bob Baxley
Veteran Design Leader

Kevin Bethune
Founder & CCO, dreams · design + life

Sarah Brooks
Design Strategist and Practical Futurist

Catherine Courage
VP UX, Consumer Products, Google

Jennifer Deitz
Director & Associate Dean,
Stanford Continuing Studies

Janice Fraser
Author of Farther, Faster, and Far Less Drama

Bob Galen
Director, Agile Practices,
Zenergy Technologies

Phil Gilbert
Retired Head of Design, IBM

Terence Gilbey
CEO, Esalen Institute

Michael Gough
Skipper & Former VP Design at Uber

Kaaren Hanson
Chief Design Officer, Consumer and
Community Banking, JPMorgan Chase

Amar Hanspal
Former Chief Product Officer
Co-CEO, Autodesk

Dave Hoffer
Design Leader

David M. Kelley
Founder, IDEO
Founder, Hasso Plattner Institute, Stanford

Thomas Kelly
Founder & CEO of Mexicue

Jennifer Kilian
Partner, McKinsey & Company

This book would be a pale version of itself without the knowledgeable and candid contributions of the following people who are learning to lead change in real time, with few role models, and under difficult circumstances. They shared the gift of their experiences and advice with us, and we are extremely grateful.

Janaki Kumar
Head of Design, Commercial Bank, JPMorgan Chase

Angela Lang
Founder, Black Leaders Organizing for Communities (BLOC)

Gene Lee
VP Experience Design, Autodesk

Jeanne Liedtka
United Technologies Professor of Business, University of Virginia Darden School of Business

John Maeda
Technologist

Justin Maguire III
Chief Design Officer, Salesforce

Jamie Myrold
Designer, Apple

Minette Norman
Founder, Minette Norman Consulting, LLC

Liz Ogbu
Founder & Principal, Studio O

Sara Ortloff
Senior Design Director, Google

Emily Pilloton-Lam
Founder & Executive Director, Girls Garage

Doug Powell
Vice President, Design Practice Management, Expedia

Ivy Ross
Vice President of Design for Hardware, Google

Christina Wodtke
Lecturer, Stanford University & Author

Sam Yen
Head of Innovation, Commercial Banking, JPMorgan Chase

Foreword

Kat Holmes
Seattle, Washington
July 2022

The idea of making a difference has a powerful allure. At an early age, I hoped to make the world kinder, safer, and healthier. If you're reading this book, you're likely also drawn to making positive changes. Many of us seek out high-complexity roles and careers in pursuit of bigger challenges that we hope will lead to a bigger impact. And many changes grow from simple beginnings, rooted in our daily experiences.

Yet, changemaking isn't a skill we apprenticed or studied. Often, it happens through experimentation. What works in one situation will fail in another. Even the most iconic changemakers in human history didn't have a clear roadmap for making these skills ubiquitous in people's lives.

In *Changemakers*, Christopher and Maria offer a powerful set of qualities for what it means to be a changemaking leader. Candid insights from a diversity of leaders make this book deeply relatable and widely applicable. Christopher and Maria interweave these voices with their own decades of hard-won lessons. Their pioneering work as systems thinkers, as women in tech, and as design-minded CEOs has eased a path for many of us to follow.

One of the greatest challenges I faced in writing *Mismatch: How Inclusion Shapes Design* was a haunting resistance to change. What makes systemic change so incredibly challenging is the human factor. It transcends multiple stakeholders and lifetimes. And let's face it, we have a lot of room to improve how humans communicate, collaborate, and build relationships. Heraclitus's eternal words "change is the only constant in life" ring true now more than ever. But change itself isn't what defeats us. It's the predictable aftershock that accompanies change: fear.

Even the mere mention of change can trigger anger, disbelief, and despair. This makes changemaking a precarious endeavor. It can be lonely and heartbreaking. But the ruthless optimism of *Changemakers* reminds us that we're never alone in our work. Fear is an expected reaction that we can equip ourselves to face. Rather than being caught on our heels, can we prepare ourselves to respond proactively to change when it's upon us?

Christopher and Maria invite us to embrace change through a human-centered perspective—one that is led by compassion and creativity. They built upon their previous book, *Rise of the DEO*, with a deeper look at how to approach any problem and opportunity as a design challenge.

The complexity that we face in the 21st century demands that we do better. The work of change must be more like a dance and less like leading an army. More like gardening and less like architecting. We must give up the urge to command and control our way through change. We must embrace progress over perfection. We must let go of pushing for the right answers and open up to asking better questions.

As Christopher and Maria say, "No one hires a design team in hopes of maintaining the status quo." And "Modern changemakers are those who would no longer treat problems as if they were fixed in time, but rather seek solutions suitable to evolving and complex circumstances."

I wish you all the best in doing this work with great hope, audacity, and care for one another.

Chapter 1

The Imperfect Future

When Neil Armstrong landed on the moon, the concept of progress was almost universally popular. Few people protested the arrival of new vaccines, faster food, advanced appliances, or more powerful cars. The envisioned future had its own neighborhood in Disneyland and popular television shows imagined even more transformations on the horizon.

In this context, "change" was synonymous with "improved." New companies were created to commercialize inventions, while older companies focused on what could be enhanced, remodeled, or extended. Ambitious graduates sought emerging fields like computer science and genetic engineering as sure paths to prosperity, and young children pretended to live in a world with flying cars and robot dogs. Underlying all this was a promise—inferred but nonetheless clear: change, and those who led it, would deliver a positive trajectory of technical, social, and organizational advancements that consistently produced benefits and left all longing for more.

Nobody is living on the moon right now, but some of the envisioned advancements arrived as promised. The 21st century started with flip phones, cable TV, and encyclopedias on CD. In barely 20 years, phones morphed into supercomputers with immediate access to near infinite knowledge. Billions of people rose up from extreme poverty, and medical advances improved life on every continent. World leaders communicate on Twitter for anyone to follow and women, people of color, and LGBTQ folks finally have a modicum of power.

This is progress by any definition, and much of it was on display in that long-ago Disney exhibit, but its trajectory has not been smooth, and its benefits are countered by unanticipated outcomes. Tech behemoths barely out of their adolescence connect the world beyond physical barriers, but also distribute a daily tsunami of misinformation and lies. People worry that their phones track them, their smart homes spy on them, and their personal data is being sold to the highest bidders. Employers are likely to reorganize every other year, and employee skill sets need constant upgrading because a replacement can come from anywhere at any time for almost any reason and may not even be human.

Change now happens so pervasively, so exponentially fast, and with such erratic impact that it is as likely to cause stress as it is to bring delight. Ask a cross section of people how they feel about change and this tension becomes evident. From those who lead change, you'll hear that it's inspiring *and* frustrating, satisfying *and* nerve-wracking. From those being changed, you'll hear that it's needed *and* threatening, beneficial *and* frightening. Unquestioning support has disappeared, along with the assumption of a positive trajectory.

But change is needed—perhaps even more and faster. It's needed for existential problems like managing climate change and morally important issues like administering social justice. Organizations need change in order to stay relevant and competitive. Institutions and communities need change to help shift them to new priorities and to embrace new tools. Governments need change to help them meet a range of challenges from economic security to environmental sustainability and more. Change is needed at all levels and in many diverse circumstances. It's needed now and in the future. Most importantly, it's needed in a way that creates more benefits than damage.

What's in the Way?

The 1960s' vision of progress as a smooth flow of relentlessly positive innovation was certainly a fairytale. It focused too keenly on optimistic outcomes and ignored challenging realities. But it is worth asking why change that's imagined and desired by so many people rarely happens as envisioned. Why do innovations disrupt and distort social norms instead of fitting seamlessly into everyone's lives? Why are business, community, and political leaders blind to obstacles that result in unintended consequences? Why are high-level goals like peace, inclusivity, and an enhanced experience of life considered out of reach?

These are deep and difficult questions to answer. Somewhere a grad student is developing robust arguments and reams of evidence supporting a well-rounded theory of how progress inevitably descends into chaos. That analysis will be enlightening, but in the meantime three obvious suspects make positive and desired transitions difficult to achieve: a fragmented world, intractable problems, and outdated approaches to making change.

A Fragmented World

When significant cultural or technological transitions take place, they often produce messy, conflict-ridden divides. Consequential advancements, like the advent of printing, electricity, or computerization, deliver significant benefits but also cause disorder and resistance as they impact people's lives. Some people learn of and adapt to a change early while others remain unaware of what's happening or actively resist adapting.

As a result, the world fractures into different segments where some people have advantages that others don't have, and some fear problems that others don't see.

It's hard to imagine an era more fragmented than this one. News, books, and media have splintered into a mosaic of perspectives that all reflect a different version of truth. A constrained set of respected thought leaders has been replaced by an army of influencers, and shared experiences are increasingly rare. At least five generations of adults compete for relevance and authority in organizational hierarchies, on moral issues, and

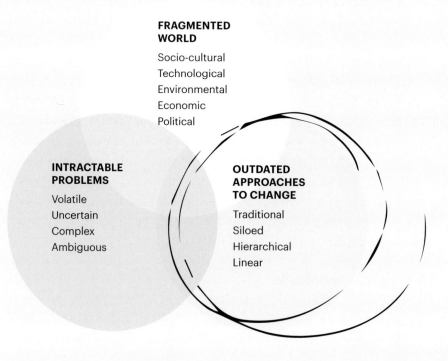

**FRAGMENTED
WORLD**

Socio-cultural
Technological
Environmental
Economic
Political

**INTRACTABLE
PROBLEMS**

Volatile
Uncertain
Complex
Ambiguous

**OUTDATED
APPROACHES
TO CHANGE**

Traditional
Siloed
Hierarchical
Linear

What's in the way?

through lifestyle choices. New definitions of gender vie for acceptance, and new recognitions of sexual preference confound traditional expectations. On a more foundational level, some world cultures are living in the 21st century, while others are barely out of the 10th. In some countries, women are regarded as equals; in others, they are equated with pets. On some roads, people drive Teslas; on others, they ride donkeys.

Fragmentation like this inevitably leads to tribal inclinations. People who think or act similarly band together and try to ignore those who are different from them. But while the formation of a tribe or sect may calm tensions, it creates an almost impermeable barrier to problem-solving because it's impossible to gain consensus. The chasm between world views is too wide to cross.

Intractable Problems

This increasingly fragmented world is also awash in problems that resist straightforward resolution. They are suitably labeled as "wicked," "untamed," or most recently "VUCA" (volatile, uncertain, complex, and ambiguous.) Where the cause of a traditional problem can be isolated and analyzed, a complex problem is linked to multiple other systems, each of which contributes new inputs and intricacies. Often, the true source of a wicked problem is hidden or misunderstood, and cause and effect are extremely difficult to identify or model. A solution may require imaginative leaps and several iterations to get right.

As technology bleeds into every aspect of life and interconnects people, their thoughts, and their things, straightforward problems become multidimensional and increasingly daunting. Solutions need to address not only the stated problem, but also its context, its connected parts, and its potential ramifications. Often in these convoluted situations the only course of action is a "best guess."

Building suspension bridges and erecting skyscrapers were feats of incredible engineering in their time, but the underlying rules of physics as they applied to construction were reasonably well-known. Compare those instances to the current development of artificial intelligence, which is being implemented before it is fully understood, or the challenge of climate change, which is exceeding the extent of scientific knowledge.

Similarly, conquering smallpox and decoding DNA required amazing ingenuity and perseverance, but the pioneers who led these pursuits had a singular goal and could count on a relatively receptive population. Compare those accomplishments with the more recent need to create a Covid vaccine. To experts, the difficulty was scientific and specific in nature: find a means of protecting humans from a deadly virus. They did it in record time, employing novel technology and admirable collaboration, but that didn't solve the problem. Additional complications branched out from the original. Some were predictable, such as how to reach people in remote areas or how to make the vaccine affordable to poorer countries. Some were not predictable, such as how to convince celebrities that the vaccine wouldn't reduce male virility or that horse paste was not a viable alternative.

There are wicked problems galore right now in all countries, among all communities, and at all levels of organizations. Governments consider whether they should pursue democracy, socialism, or authoritarianism, and whether cryptocurrency should become the foundation of all transactions. Activists debate whether populations should be compensated for past discrimination and whether women's rights are negotiable. Organizations struggle to decide if work should be done remotely, how to manage diversity, and whether to take sides in political disputes. These and countless more problems vex advocates of change because their root causes are dimensional, their connections are widespread, and their solutions are convoluted. Any remedies will have upsides and downsides. They will have people in favor and people opposed. Even carefully plotted solutions will produce unanticipated consequences.

Outdated Approaches to Change

Contrary to what some people think, significant or systemic change doesn't just happen in the course of normal life. Minor change can occur quickly and relatively easily if a need is urgent enough or an opportunity rich enough. But more notable change requires extensive effort, substantial resources, and highly capable leadership. In business, it follows a process or a specific approach endorsed by change management specialists who frame the way an organization defines and implements any desired transformation. Interestingly, these approaches tend to reflect the function or specialty that businesses valued most at that time.

For example, when Disneyland showcased progress in the 1960s, the approach to change endorsed by most executives mirrored a mid-century emphasis on manufacturing: change was carefully planned and precisely executed in an assembly line fashion. To modify anything meant to "freeze" the current state, make the revision, and then "unfreeze" it. Leaders were similar to military commanders. Whatever top executives decided, everyone else had to follow.

When companies shifted from manufacturing to service offerings in the 1980s, finance became the dominant function. Change was newly branded as "re-engineering," and was sought as a way to improve capital allocation and increase per-share value. Leaders were strategic visionaries. Top executives still made most decisions, but employees wanted to follow them so as to not get left behind.

Corporate and social attitudes toward change management morphed again in the 1990s, as the web spread beyond Silicon Valley. Echoing

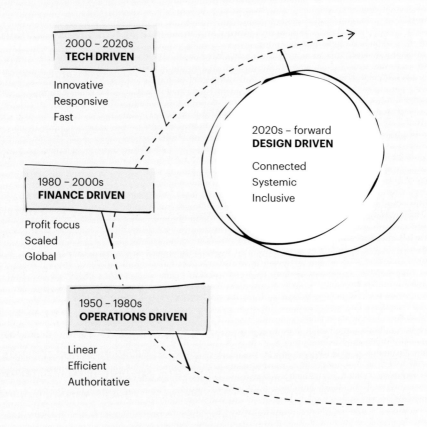

The process of making change evolves

the attributes of startup culture, companies were birthed in garages, and products were created overnight. Change became innovation—a concept that promised to renovate tired companies into transformative juggernauts capable of keeping up with the dizzying pace of technological growth and global competition. Leaders were inventive renegades who moved fast and broke things. Everyone else hoped they could be like them.

Each of these different approaches to making change depended on the tools and mental models common to corporations and their dominant business function at the time. Each new proposal developed different philosophies and theories of how to help people adjust and how to ensure that the envisioned outcomes turned out as planned. As a new method gained popularity, it escaped corporate confines and influenced all change initiatives, including those of communities, nonprofits, and governments. For a while each had some success. But notably, each approach began to lose its dominance and relevance as the times, the tools, and the techniques changed.

That's happening now and it's adding to the conflict and confusion of a fragmented world with intractable problems. Most organizations and communities continue to push change in a siloed, top-down manner, ignoring the social, educational, and technological shifts that have made people more independent and less willing to blindly follow leaders. Outdated approaches to change remain rigid and rule-bound, despite technology that enables expansive connectivity and fluid communication. While popular culture and younger generations emphasize the importance of empathy and inclusion, entities fail to consider how improvements for some might worsen situations for others. They rush experimentation, turning invention into a contest where the biggest and boldest initiative wins, regardless of what is lost in the race.

The misalignment between the desire for change and the inability to deliver it successfully leaves individuals struggling to understand their role and responsibility in the process. Empowered and overinformed by the web, cell phones, and social media, many people lack any training on how to use these gifts effectively. In an effort to contribute, they spread their thoughts like seeds, casting ideas and complaints broadly across networks, hoping to land on fertile soil. Others give up and retreat. They consign the future to forces beyond their control, crediting a deity, science, historical precedent, or random luck. With no role to play, their only responsibility is to warn or critique and hope for more favorable trends.

Little improvement is possible if leaders and the teams that support them continue to promote change haphazardly and impulsively as though everything is a startup. Nor is there any benefit attained when people assume they have no power to alter course and resign themselves to whatever happens. In a fragmented world struggling with complex challenges, the current approaches to making change have largely stopped working.

What's Next?

The transitional era fragmenting the world has only begun. People everywhere are still digesting the impacts of the internet, and it's about to be served up artificial intelligence, virtual reality, and a whole new version of the web. Climate change, the needs of emerging populations, global conflicts, and the god-like powers of gene-editing will provide a steady stream of new complexities. These conditions are impossible to ignore or to modify, but how change is implemented is a choice and there's some early evidence of how it might be evolving.

Startup culture is still popular, and innovation is still a potent buzzword, but respect for authoritative, top-down approaches is losing favor to laterally connected, distributed collaborations. Wealthy tech gurus are still idolized, but so are humbler, values-driven leaders who spur collective action. Strategy documents are shrinking to the size of posters, and detailed plans are being diminished by an explosion of experimentation. These developments, along with the actions of some early movers, hint at the future of changemaking.

Chef José Andrés noted the patterns of poor disaster relief response amid an abundance of underutilized food resources. He tried to work within existing hierarchical structures, but quickly realized that the problems were often due to the regulations and bureaucracies that enforced them. As an alternative, he founded World Central Kitchen, and led an ad hoc community of chefs and food providers to rapidly focus resources exactly where needed without hierarchies, strategic plans, or ROI concerns. He continues to iterate, learning from failures or flaws.

Black Lives Matter united a like-minded, but highly diverse population of activists, with no headquarters, no central planning, and no official leader. Noting that nothing had changed despite decades of promises, they identified the problem of invisibility and found ways to gain attention. Using social media, they united powerful coalitions of people who shared the same experiences and frustrations. Their collective action has prompted more change in response to systemic racism than traditional organizations pursuing that identical goal for over a hundred years.

Web3 is being developed by a devoted crowd of entrepreneurs, engineers, and community leaders working together to shape the future of the internet. Ridiculed by some as naïve and delusional, they are steadily building a distributed, iterative assemblage of networks with the potential to disrupt and reorder nearly everything. The loose collection of believers building this space have noted people's growing desire for transparency, distributed ownership, and authentication. They share an appreciation for the problems that technology has created and seek to address them by working collaboratively in different roles and with different approaches, iterating as they go. The ecosystem they are building is nascent, but its potential has attracted some of the brightest minds of this generation and earned massive venture investment.

None of these organizations are perfect in the expression of their vision or execution, but each is making change in a new and significant way that's worth unpacking. Each of these examples suggests a new approach to organizational or community change that suits the time and fits the evolutionary trajectory of corporate change management. These are approaches that don't slow change down but ensure a higher quality outcome. They leverage newly connected communities and help people channel their passion and ability. These approaches pursue methodologies that encourage a deeper appreciation of people and their perspectives. They embrace processes that pay attention to potential downsides. They offer an improved approach to change that uses the tools and technology needed to build an inclusive future that works for more than just those in charge.

These real-time instances of how to make change in today's world are further bolstered by early insights from Bill Drayton, the founder of Ashoka, an organization that helped define the social entrepreneur movement. His thoughts captured the value of these recent examples and spurred our thinking about what this new approach to change might demand in terms of leadership and process. Drayton described modern changemakers as those who would no longer treat problems as if they were fixed in time, but rather seek solutions suitable to evolving and complex circumstances. In 2006, he defined this new breed of change leaders as

People who can see the patterns around them, identify the problems in any situation, figure out ways to solve the problem, organize fluid teams, lead collective action, and then continually adapt as situations change.

He called these people "changemakers," an apt title for those capable of building a more desirable future amid an increasingly complex and irrational world. But while the title is new, the description is familiar. It is a close approximation of how good design leaders think and behave, whether they are changing a graphic, a platform, or an institution.

Designing Change

"Design" is an ambitiously flexible word. It can mean a dozen different things as a noun and another dozen as a verb. It refers to both a process and its end result. To design can include doing, making, having, seeing, or formulating. A design can be a thing, a place, an interface, or an experience. It can be done by businesses, households, schoolchildren, even nature.

In this context, where it is central to change, it means to develop a future state or condition in concert with those affected by it.

This is a mindset and capability increasingly adopted by large organizations seeking to survive and thrive in a rapidly evolving world. While manufacturing, finance, and innovative zeal still matter to organizations, the function currently taking center stage is design. Apple, the world's most valuable company, began touting the value of design in the 1990s. For a while, it was the only technology firm courageous enough to bet its business on this claim. But when cell phones, social media, and the cloud began connecting everyone, the world's attention shifted from a singular focus on technological features to one that included the user's experience of technology. It was not enough for phones and apps to work; they also had to be desirable and intuitive. That required design.

As digital connections wrapped the world, the corporate move to design-driven innovation gained urgency. IBM conveyed legitimacy by hiring thousands of designers as part of reorienting its business. Facebook and Google flooded their campuses with UX and UI designers. Nearly every large consulting firm bought a design firm to augment its offerings, and companies everywhere hired at least one designer—if only to say they were design-driven. This transition continues to benefit every design school graduate and many who have converted from other fields, and it shows no signs of slowing.

Elevating design from a task to a strategy shifts perspective. Problems become opportunities and customers or stakeholders become important contributors in the search for viable solutions. Experimentation, captured in renderings, comps, hypotheses, and trial balloons, mitigates risk. Iteration delivers refinement and failure offers guidance. Imagination rises to the same lofty height as analysis, and intuition is no longer just guesswork. The strategic use of design respects the context, constraints, and requirements of business but marries them with the abstraction and openness of creativity. Most importantly, it recognizes that authoritative directives are more a hindrance than a help, and that the most innovative solutions arise from diverse collaborations, not singular dictates.

A Modern Mindset

Design provokes and responds to change. No one hires a design team with the goal of keeping everything the same. Designs enter the fray when a problem needs to be solved or something needs to be improved. Good designers become adept at identifying benefits in change. They can imagine a better way to communicate, a simpler means of creating engagement, or a different function that addresses a hidden problem. As a result, they are more comfortable with change as a continual flow in their life. Each new client, new tool, new material, or new perspective represents the possibility of positive change.

Design is famously useful in addressing issues that are ill-defined, unknown, or insanely complex. Perhaps because designers are trained to see every challenge as a problem that can be solved, they've developed tools, techniques, and processes that help them uncover insights, experiment and prototype, and deliver clear, valued results, regardless of the context. They push to look beyond what's expected or what's been done before, connecting to novel approaches and ideas.

In addition to embracing change and thriving on tough problems, design is collaborative. Few designers work alone. They have clients, customers, or colleagues. Depending on the assignment, they engage with engineers, authors, suppliers, coders, color experts, and more. Equally important, designers expect and accept feedback on their work. They include the input of others in their creative process. While some designers may prefer to dominate collaborations or work alone, that's a remnant of the past that is rapidly becoming the exception. Most are comfortable as contributors, taking the lead when their expertise is most relevant and following others when it's not.

Lastly, but of equal importance, design is "human-focused," meaning it is squarely focused on the behaviors, beliefs, and motivations of real people. Decades before neuroscience confirmed the importance of understanding people's mental and emotional states to connect and communicate better with them, designers were interviewing, surveying, and observing people in all aspects of their lives. They do this because a design only succeeds if people adopt it.

Given these attributes, it's not much of a stretch to suggest that design's power and prowess can be extended from making products, services, and experiences to making change in an era struggling with fragmented perspectives and complex problems. Treating the future as a design space is a viable approach. Using the processes common to design is an appropriate choice. Employing the tools and techniques that designers value allows new perspectives and enables more creative solutions.

Designing the future doesn't mean swapping out MBAs for MFAs or shifting from learning statistics to learning to draw. It means adopting a practical, beneficial framework that encourages and incorporates diverse input and creative output. It means embracing change as a constant and directing it toward a carefully considered purpose, weighted to benefit the people most impacted.

Why This Book?

As your authors and guides on this journey, we have a deep familiarity and respect for designers and their abilities. We each ran successful, independent design firms in Silicon Valley for over 25 years starting in the 1990s. We led research, development, and execution of design projects for startups, nonprofits, community services, government agencies, academic institutions, and hundreds of large corporations. We also regularly transformed our own practices, shifting from a focus on graphic design to experience design, from press visits to Zoom calls, from printed page to VR environments.

We led change relentlessly for our teams and our clients throughout every decade, always cognizant of its cost and doing our best to make sure that we weren't leading others off a cliff. We made countless mistakes and learned a lifetime of lessons. We also benefited from others pursuing similar goals in different companies, many of whom shared their experience and wisdom with us as we created this book. We appreciate their generosity and include many of their observations and advice in the chapters ahead.

We no longer lead teams exploring what's possible or building experiences on the latest technology platforms. Others have assumed those roles, and we actively support and coach them. Our role now is to share what we know, to pass forward what we gained in those 25 plus years of designing change, and hopefully to stimulate a new appreciation of what design can do.

Perhaps the Disney version of progress was naïve, but its opposite is worse. To cling to the past and refuse to change is to invite atrophy and eventually fade from relevance. Smooth progress with no bumps along the way is unlikely, but none can afford to simply shrug their shoulders and accept a future that spins increasingly out of control. The future can't be a perfect expression of a meticulously calibrated vision. There are too many unforeseeable variables for that type of optimism. But there's a lot of middle ground between unmanageable chaos and godlike manifestation. It's that middle space that seems attainable—a balance between the rigid funk of stagnation and the craziness of chaos.

For these reasons and others that we'll explore in this book, we anticipate that the next approach to change will be design-driven, and its leaders—at all levels and in a wide range of circumstances—will be changemakers.

These changemakers will be people who can view the future of communities, companies, and even countries as a design problem: an opportunity space that can be clearly defined, intentionally studied, and reliably addressed. That's the goal of this book—to describe the leaders and approaches appropriate for this time and its uniquely complex challenges, and to encourage those who can make change to act in the right way, in the right place, and with the right support.

Takeaways

The future needs help.
Fast-paced and chaotic change has divided the world. Partly this is due to the messiness and fragmentation common to transitional eras, the increasing complexity of problems and challenges, and outdated approaches to making change.

A new approach to change is emerging.
To progress in a more inclusive and less damaging way, the traditional approach of top-down change needs to be replaced by an approach that is based on a deeper understanding of people and problems, which tries to anticipate and adapt to potential downsides, and encourages cooperation and partnership.

Design—in its broadest definition—fits this need.
Design provokes and responds to change, is famously useful in addressing issues that are ill-defined or insanely complex, and is almost always collaborative. It empowers human-focused solutions and is increasingly accepted as the preferred approach to innovation.

Take It Further

Changing on the Job: Developing Leaders for a Complex World.
Jennifer Garvey Berger. Stanford Business Books, 2011.

Complexity: The Emerging Science at the Edge of Order and Chaos.
M. Mitchell Waldrop. Simon & Schuster, 1992.

How to Change: The Science of Getting from
Where You Are to Where You Want to Be.
Katy Milkman. Portfolio, 2021.

Living with Complexity.
Donald A. Norman. The MIT Press, 2010.

No Ordinary Disruption: The Four
Global Forces Breaking All the Trends.
R. Dobbs, J. Manyika, and J. Woetzel. PublicAffairs, 2015.

Start with Why: How Great Leaders
Inspire Everyone to Take Action.
Simon Sinek. Portfolio, 2009.

Switch: How to Change Things When Change Is Hard.
Chip and Dan Heath. Crown Business, 2010.

Why Design Matters: Conversations with the
World's Most Creative People.
Debbie Millman. Harper Design, 2022.

Chapter 2

Becoming a Changemaker

Becoming a changemaker starts with understanding change. "Change" is as difficult to define as "design" is. Both are all-encompassing words that can be applied to something as simple as a preferred brand of toothpaste or as profound as religious expressions. Change can be done to others, with others, for others, or alone. It can be directed, seduced, led, or incentivized. It can be a visible action, such as changing your shirt, or mostly hidden, such as changing your mind. It can be short-term and variable, or long-term and lasting. Despite its loose definition and broad application, it always carries the threat of drama and the promise of new.

On these pages, to "make change" means to drive a systemic transformation of something from its current state to a more preferred one by adopting the mindset, the frameworks, and the techniques common to design. It implies progress, although not necessarily in a straight line or as originally conceived. It requires intent, action, and leadership in some form. It cannot be forced from a position of authority or sustained without widespread acceptance.

A starting point is identifying the motivations and qualities common to effective changemakers, such as those highlighted in the previous chapter. These inclinations are important because changemakers need to inspire and unite others to achieve a shared purpose and vision. They extend their reach and impact by connecting with like-minded people through the core of who they are and what they believe. They use their purpose and values to guide actions and sustain support through uncertainty. They rely on their courage to take bets and overcome obstacles. The leadership skills and natural charisma sufficient in earlier eras remain important for changemakers to develop, but they're no longer enough.

Purpose

Becoming a changemaker starts with purpose—what you want to change. We can't fully imagine how wide-ranging this intent may be, but we can speculate on its variety. A changemaker can be

A designer with ambition to play a role in a company's decision-making

A young professional looking for more meaningful responsibilities

A skilled craftsperson interested in building community

A rising activist who longs for more impact

A talented and experienced retiree with plenty of energy but no place to apply it

"Purpose" can be specific to who you are, or it can be more general and outcome oriented. For example, a changemaker could want to help a community become more cohesive and aligned. Or find a fairer approach to allocating resources. Or a better method of coordinating different functions within an organization. A changemaker could strive to invigorate a declining town or improve a small business. Whatever the specifics, a changemaker's purpose is to initiate and make positive, systemic change, even if they aren't currently assigned that responsibility.

Strengths, training, and experience are important, but purpose is in the driver's seat. It contributes to authority and legitimacy more than position or title because it explains where you are headed and what you want to accomplish. It stimulates a hunger for knowledge and a willingness to consider the unconventional. It serves as an effective litmus test for those interested in working with you. If they don't share your purpose, there's no fit.

Purpose alone is insufficient. In fact, a changemaker driven solely by purpose can be disruptive and ineffective. But it is the keystone trait uniting all other attributes. Without it, a changemaker has no focus or drive. Two closely linked traits—courage and optimism—add to purpose and begin to round out a changemaker's capabilities. Both characteristics are genetically determined to some extent, but each can be learned and strengthened.

Courage

A clear intent to make positive change can initiate action, but only if accompanied by the courage to act on that intent. While the stock image of courage is a lone man approaching an insurmountable challenge, that's outdated and inadequate for most situations. The test of courage is not a solo act, nor is it as simple as facing tough odds. Courage is an everyday act, particularly in making change.

Becoming a changemaker requires becoming comfortable with change—not once a year or even every few months—but constantly, as a natural part of life. It takes courage to suggest that change is needed; to resist the ease of conventional perspectives and assumptions and welcome new directions. It takes courage to live with ambiguity and contradiction, while advocating for the effectiveness of imagination and intuition. It takes courage to stay open to diverse opinions, to accept pushback, to field endless questions, and to face additional complications.

As many have noted, courage is not the absence of fear. Rather it's the ability to move forward despite the fear you feel. It means overcoming anxiety and worry in order to step out of your comfort zone. It means risking failure and rejection in order to be more creative. Courage braves hidebound bureaucracies and hidden saboteurs. It risks ridicule by advocating for an idea that others dismiss or calling for change that others don't envision. Courage provides the backbone to do what you believe is right, even though it might get you fired.

While courage is an important asset of a changemaker, developing it is a big lift. It's easy to be in favor of change at a conceptual level, but at a personal level it triggers fear.

Humans are risk-sensing organisms with brains programmed to notice the slightest deviation and quickly assess whether it is beneficial or not. As neuroscientist Lisa Feldman Barrett[1] explained, the brain is constantly constructing concepts from past experiences as a hypothesis of what will happen next. If what your body senses matches what your brain predicts, all is well. But if your body senses anything different from what your brain predicts—in other words, a change—the limbic system goes on alert. If the brain judges the change as a threat, it triggers the "fight, flight, or freeze" response.

The shift to fight, flight, or freeze is not subtle or rational. That's largely because when the brain is on alert, it uses up oxygen and glucose,

---

1. A detailed listing of Dr. Barrett's work can be found on her website, lisafeldman barrett.com.

siphoning those resources from the parts of the brain that could make more refined judgments. As a result, your more logical thinking abilities are impaired just when they would be most helpful. This instinctual system no doubt served humans well in prehistoric times, helping nomadic peoples avoid carnivores and hostile tribes, but in our current environment, it often acts more as a foe than a friend. Even if reason reveals the possibility of positive outcomes, your neurons are hard-wired to sense and respond quickly to any hint of danger. In a matchup between reason and instinct, instinct usually wins. You ignore the benefits that change can bring and stick with what's familiar.

Biologically based fear cannot be vanquished, but ironically it can be used to help build courage. Fear is an entry point for exploring its cause and benefiting from that exploration. If fear prompts a re-examination of risks, it can help build confidence in your decision or redirect your efforts. If fear makes you slow down and explore other options, you might uncover more opportunities. Rather than thinking of fear as a cliff you need to jump off or a wall you need to burst through, think of it as a partner that can co-pilot change with you. Make fear the first "member" of your team with the assigned role of helping increase your courage.

Optimism

Optimism sustains courage and purpose by continually reframing what's possible in a way that encourages and directs further effort. It makes change more desirable by pointing relentlessly to a positive outcome, a future state better than the current one.

Sadly, optimism suffers from bad PR. It's associated with a blindness to downsides and a superficial cheeriness that sees only sunny skies. While it can contribute to inexpert actions, like underestimating resistance or missing key obstacles, healthy optimism is not naïve. It's an intelligent and success-enabling belief that sees failures as temporary setbacks capable of correction. Used appropriately, it conveys a feeling of agency over the future—that potential outcomes are dependent on changes undertaken today. Optimism doesn't ignore reality or deny the existence of evil or ill-intent, but it counters those forces with a firm belief in humans' unlimited capacity to make positive, lasting change. It further assumes that people are collectively good and willing to work together to achieve those better outcomes and to overcome the hurdles in their way.

Research from another respected neuroscientist, Tali Sharot,[2] found that most people (approximately 80%) are born with an optimistic bias. Interestingly, this inherent benefit largely disappears when you feel threatened or when you are taking in too much negative information. It's resuscitated by recasting the threat as one that you can overcome. It's enhanced by viewing positive results as permanent and the consequence of strengths, and viewing negative outcomes as temporary, remedied by learning and trying again.

Optimism combines with courage and purpose to provide a rational, determined sense of where you're going and a positive commitment to get there. They outline the scope and intent of your ambition, but they're enhanced and colored by qualities that are a bit less linear and a bit more abstract: passion, values, and integrity.

Passion

Passion is an emotional commitment that fuels long hours of work, constant attention to detail, and a continual desire for more information, more opportunity, and more exploration. Identifying whether or not you

---

2. A detailed listing of Dr. Sharot's work can be found on her website, www.ucl.ac.uk /pals/research/experimental-psychology/person/dr-tali-sharot/.

are passionate about a purpose or intention can be as easy as answering the question "Do I really truly care about this?" The world desperately needs talented professionals to lead communities dealing with a warming climate, but if this doesn't excite you, then it's not your passion. The world may have more than enough legal minds, but if pursuing lawful remedies to injustice is what gets you out of bed in the morning, your passion could distinguish you from the crowd. Your organization may not appreciate the value of a new technology, but if adopting it excites you, your passion could drive its eventual acceptance.

Another clear indication of passion is what you're willing to sacrifice. To follow your passion, are you willing to take a cut in pay? Are you willing to get a degree or spend hours getting certified? Are you comfortable doing the most work for the least credit? The more willing you are to give up time, effort, money, or ego, the stronger your passion's hold is, and the more powerful it can be when paired with the appropriate purpose, skills, and environment.

A passionate determination to persevere despite the costs goes by the punchy name of "grit." Grit helps you stick to the intent you have, even

Terry Gilbey
CEO Esalen Institute

If anybody embarks on leadership in a change environment and is doing it for any other purpose than to see the outcomes, they're going to walk away pretty dissatisfied, particularly in environments of significant change. It is a thankless task. It is a role in which you spend all of your time apologizing, but nobody apologizes to you. You can never have friendships in an organization where you're driving change. You can be friendly, but you can't ever let it get to the level of friendship. It's brutal, it's hard thankless work, and everybody wants to see you fail.

So if you're going to embark upon significant organizational change as a leader, you've got to be darn sure you're committed, and you don't care about what it's going to take to do it. That's the cost of doing it. You will lose friends, you will lose respect, you will lose colleagues, you will lose sleep, you will lose weight, you will gain respect, you will gain friends, you will gain colleagues. And at the end of the day, the only person that can judge if you are successful or not is yourself. So you better have a really strong internal locus of control. ▲

when the effort or struggles make it barely tolerable. It's what focuses you on making small, iterative changes, steadfastly believing that these mostly invisible improvements will compound and yield value over time. Like most traits, grit is genetic to some extent, but it also can be nurtured. Interestingly, research indicates that grit is not related to talent. Like optimism, it's more compatible with having a "growth mindset," the belief that you can learn and grow with effort.

A close companion of grit, and another feature of passion, is "resilience." Resilience helps you bounce back from adversity. It is the ability to absorb shocks or loss and rebound stronger. Think of widely admired leaders or changemakers. If you look at the full trajectory of their lives, it's likely littered with failures. Steve Jobs was fired from Apple. Barack Obama lost his first run for Congress. Olympic athletes and professional sports teams often lose as many competitions as they win. Scientists' failure to success ratio can be 1,000:1 or worse. What makes these people successful isn't their lack of failure or minimal downfalls. What makes them successful is their resilience. They get up and try again. Why? Often it's because of their passion, as founder and CEO of Mexicue, Thomas Kelly, explained:

> *If you truly love what you do it makes things alot easier. I started with a co-founder who had entrepreneurial grit and was excited about starting a business. But he didn't have the passion for food that I do, and that became a problem because it's just not a quick path to success. It's a long path, and you have to really, really love it. After a few years of the grind of doing what we do, my co-founder moved on to do something else. But for me, that grind has been not just tolerable, it's been enjoyable. Because I really love food and hospitality.*

True passion like Thomas's can arm you with an abundance of grit and resilience and can attract like-minded people. That's an important advantage because changemaking is a group sport. It requires a coalition of the willing in order to have any chance of success. The next step—connecting with them and sustaining their support—benefits from a foundation of shared values and clearly demonstrated integrity.

Values

Passion is shaped and refined by personal values that motivate and guide behavior. They influence your stance on topics and nudge how you react to them. When consistent, they help explain why you act in a particular way, attracting the support of like-minded people and helping to steer group decision-making. Values are highly subjective, and there's no exact catalog of changemaker values, but there are some values that complement and reinforce actions changemakers *need* to take. Honesty, transparency, and trustworthiness aid in building coalitions and deepening support. Fairness and acceptance support diverse voices and divergent input. Openness facilitates creativity.

Being aware of your values and their relative importance is as essential as knowing your strengths and weaknesses. But to become trusted, values need to be demonstrated through actions. You confirm and strengthen your values whenever you use them. This might mean saying "no" to a request that crosses a personal boundary, regardless of the consequences. It could mean voicing your objection, even though you are in the minority. It might include defining and enforcing an acceptable workload, modeling preferred forms of feedback and communication, or owning up to mistakes.

Conflict and distrust can arise when values are not evident or seem overly variable. While values can be flexible, or dependent on circumstances and trade-offs, those that remain unchanged over time provide stability to others. When others know your values and see your commitment to them, their psychological security is boosted. They are reassured by the promise of constancy in the midst of uncertainty. This steadiness doesn't end conflict, but it can make it more reasonable and productive.

Integrity

Having integrity means living in accordance with your values. It means taking stands and actions that are aligned with your values or revising those values to stay in harmony with your actions. Values can and should develop as you learn and grow. But even as they evolve, they need to remain consistent with your actions to be believable and steadfast, as Liz Ogbu, founder of Studio O, shared:

> *I make it very clear with everyone that I will walk away if we reach a point where the project no longer represents our values.... I don't think that's something we're taught in school. I think the system is set up to say you're a failure if you walk away; you're a failure if this thing didn't work. But some things were not meant to be, and some things aren't aligned. You can only produce this sort of change if the conditions are appropriate for it.*

If you lead systemic change, you don't have the luxury of tossing off phrases like "it's business, not personal," or "this is just how it's done," as excuses for decisions you don't personally endorse. If you're thinking this sounds like New Age feminist bullshit, let us be clearer. We are not saying that changemakers need to conform to select values or demonstrate some level of goodness. We are saying that values represent a significant aspect of a changemaker's appeal and influence, and they can't be easily ignored when it's inconvenient to follow them.

Most transformations led by changemakers will be dependent on values in one way or another. For example, you may want to revolutionize journalism by eliminating its dependence on advertising, and your values may be squarely aligned with that outcome. But then research shows you that advertising is the most efficient and democratic means of supporting journalism for a diverse and far-reaching audience. If you act on this insight and shift your support to advertising, you must realign your values with that decision. If you don't, your values are no longer trustable. You can stick with your original values and ignore the research, or you can act on the research and modify your values. Either choice is reasonable, but whichever one you make is a confirmation of your values and proof of your integrity.

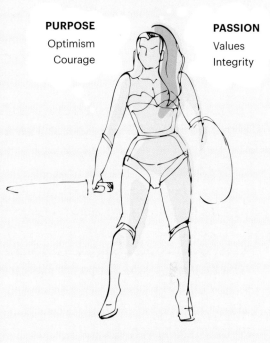

PURPOSE
Optimism
Courage

PASSION
Values
Integrity

Purpose and passion

These qualities—your purpose and your passion, your courage and optimism, your values and integrity—are necessary qualities for embracing and navigating the challenges of making systemic change. Developing them is similar to building muscles and flexibility. You won't be buff or agile in a day, a week, or even a month. But repeated practice will strengthen them and improve your ability to make and lead change in an environment that is open to it.

Takeaways

Determine your purpose and passion.

Purpose is a clearly articulated intent or goal. Passion is an emotional commitment that fuels long hours of work, constant attention to detail, and a continual desire for more information, more opportunity, and more exploration. Both are essential changemaker qualities.

Use courage and optimism to overcome resistance.

A changemaker must be comfortable with change—not once a year or even every few months—but constantly, as a natural part of life. Optimism boosts courage by continually reframing what's possible in a way that encourages and directs further effort.

Clarify values and demonstrate integrity.

Values influence your stance on topics, guide your behavior, attract like-minded people, and steer group decision-making. They confirm or undercut your integrity.

Take It Further

A Liberated Mind: How to Pivot Toward What Matters.
Stephen C. Hayes. Avery, 2019.

Change: How Organizations Achieve Hard-to-Imagine Results in Uncertain and Volatile Times.
John P. Kotter. Wiley, 2021.

Change Makers Podcast
(changemakers.works)

Elastic: Flexible Thinking in a Time of Change.
Leonard Mlodinow. Pantheon, 2018.

Grit: The Power of Passion and Perseverance.
Angela Duckworth. Scribner, 2016.

How Emotions Are Made: The Secret Life of the Brain.
Lisa Feldman Barrett. Mariner Books, 2017.

The Art of Resilience: Strategies for an Unbreakable Mind and Body.
Ross Edgley. HarperCollins, 2020.

The Optimism Bias: A Tour of the Irrationally Positive Brain.
Tali Sharot. Vintage, 2012.

Chapter 3

Finding a Fit

Purpose and passion long for opportunity. Change-makers who tackle problems truly suited to them leverage their competence, enhance their authority, and build their credibility. In short, their impact is amplified. Like startup founders looking for market fit, a changemaker's likelihood of success is directly related to how good this matchup is.

Market fit happens when a product perfectly matches an existing need. It's considered the "Holy Grail" of development because it greatly improves the chance of success. A similar fit—between the competence of a changemaker and the need for change—affords the same benefit. But finding this fit is difficult. A multitude of problems and challenges cry out for changemakers. These challenges take purpose and passion, but also require competence and experience relevant to the problem and a setting and culture that is open to change. On-the-job training is not a wise accommodation.

Unfortunately, those with the prerequisite skills to lead effective transitions often end up in situations that can't accept their help because change is easy to request but difficult to allow. Examples abound of changemaker skills misaligned to a problem or a setting. A changemaker hired for her creativity is later criticized for being too innovative by the old-style bank that sought her out. A changemaker acclaimed for her novel approach to education is rejected for not conforming to the community's traditional standards. A changemaker noted for his unique perspective is ignored because he's proposing something unfamiliar.

When there's alignment between the abilities and intent of a change-maker and the organization or opportunity in need of transformation, change is still a struggle, but it's not insurmountable. It's still complex and challenging, but less time is spent repeatedly fighting for attention or support. There's a decreased need to re-establish legitimacy after each pivot or small failure. Being dismissed by a new leader or sabotaged by an unhappy manager is less likely. Hurdles remain, but they are challenges related to the problem, not the people or the setting. Finding this alignment takes an honest assessment of capabilities and competence and their importance to the problem, and an unstinting appraisal of an organization or culture's openness to change.

The Right Problem

While changemakers' competence is often broad and transferable to a range of challenges, the ideal situation is where their abilities are core to solving the problem at hand and their experience is highly relevant. You may be a kick-ass executive, but that doesn't make you an effective community builder. Similarly, you may have raised millions to eradicate childhood cancer, but you might collapse under the normal daily routine of an entrepreneur. While the admonition to "fake it 'til you make it" is exhorted proudly and frequently, it's a dangerous move for a change-maker because it erodes integrity and undermines trust. A better mantra would emphasize the importance of finding a fit for your current capabilities that doesn't depend on deceit.

Table stakes for finding this fit is determining what strengths and competence you bring to an organization. When clearly and honestly identified, skills and experience help others understand what expertise a change-maker can offer and how he or she can best contribute. It initiates connection and reliance.

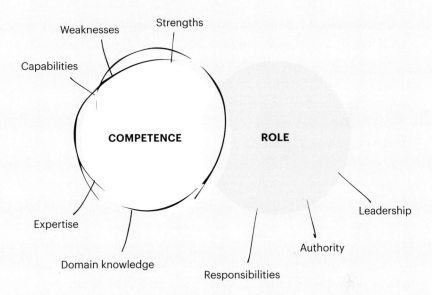

Choosing the right problem

Competence

Those who lead change are asking others to follow them in a risky under-taking. Bold, progressive ambition, no matter how passionate, can't make up for a lack of targeted ability and appropriate experience. You may be born with notable talents, but they only become strengths from practice, application, and testing. It's not enough to believe you are strategic, or to say you are practical—strengths need to be demonstrated repeatedly and consistently. They need to be capabilities on which others can rely.

Strengths are heightened by domain knowledge, or the wisdom acquired over time in a particular discipline or industry, usually through numerous failures and triumphs. To have domain knowledge means to understand the business context of the change in a broad and deep manner, as Phil Gilbert, retired head of design for IBM Corporation, relayed:

> *I had to understand the business and the business impact, irre-spective of design and design thinking and product simplifi-cation and portfolio simplification. This is a business, and if you've got banking client X, Y, or Z with a half a billion-dollar infrastructure deal in the pipeline, and you go piss them off because you want to save $12 million of development costs, that's not a sound decision.*

A changemaker with domain knowledge can act almost instinctively because they recognize the elements and patterns of a problem and its significance. In some instances, this type of competence can be gen-eralized. For example, if your experience in financial markets taught you that people act irrationally when they are frightened, that knowl-edge will probably be just as valid in a more general application. But in many cases, domain knowledge is a specific awareness that doesn't transfer easily.

Determining whether your competence and domain knowledge is a fit for an opportunity to make change starts by reviewing your strengths and weaknesses. Everyone, regardless of occupation or phase of life, has strengths. Recent high school grads can do research. Stay-at-home par-ents can manage unruly groups and counsel confused teenagers. Retired executives still know how to draft a strategy, manage a project, and coach a colleague. These strengths have been built from experience and can include a wide range of skills, aptitude, habits, emotional traits, coping behaviors, and more.

Everyone also has weaknesses, and they are as important to delineate as strengths are. Despite their ragged image, weaknesses are not necessarily personal flaws or inadequacies. They define your identity and distinguish you from others as much as strengths do, but in a different way. In many cases, they are simply the flip side of strengths. Your pronounced ability to concentrate may make you oblivious to emotional cues. Your well-developed presentation skill may have come at the cost of a more developed analytic capability.

Notably, strengths and weaknesses do not have absolute values that can be scored on a 1-10 scale. The values of strengths and weaknesses are relative compared to others. To truly be a strength, your abilities have to be better than those of others on your team or in your community. You may be an excellent analyst, but if another person is more experienced and skilled than you, your strength in this area is less valuable.

Being cognizant of these strengths and weaknesses and how they map to the opportunity for change paves the way to the best possible version of yourself by letting you concentrate on what you can do best rather than what you will struggle to accomplish. Being aware of your strengths and weaknesses, and sharing them with others, increases connection and trust and helps you find partners who can fill those gaps.

Leveling Up

Matching your competence with a suitable opportunity reinforces confidence, particularly if the match puts you in the right role. Roles imply a set of responsibilities and a level of authority. If a role is too junior for a person's competence, he or she will soon become bored and distracted. If a role is too senior, it raises anxiety and stress. In either state, the changemaker won't have the sureness to lead or contribute effectively. Finding the right role takes some trial and error and it's generally a progression, as design leader Dave Hoffer clarified:

If you're a young designer, you know your tools, you under-stand your craft, and you can describe the gestalt of the things that you're designing. As you level up, you incorporate user needs—the emotion and the empathy that is required to make a meaningful product. The next level up is being able to translate your design acumen to the way in which the business runs.

This is a thoughtful perspective on where and how to lead, and it's as applicable to changemakers as it is to designers. In the early stages of a career, changemakers can lead projects related to their specific expertise. For example, if you're a talented engineer, you may want to use that skill by joining a team assigned to change an internal process. Setting clear boundaries and expectations, for what you can and can't do, could make this a relatively sane and satisfying way to contribute.

With maturity and experience, a changemaker can start to lead in situations where multiple skills and diverse inputs are combined and leveraged. This is the essence of project management, and it's a valuable training ground for developing the ability to merge viewpoints, capabilities, and personalities. If you have experience interpreting research findings, moderating decisions, and making presentations, you may be ready to lead a small functional team with complementary skills.

When a changemaker's expertise and knowledge extend to a full awareness of how the organization or community functions, he or she is ready for a more strategic leadership role. This role requires a sophisticated grasp of trade-offs, future goals, and stakeholder politics. It rests on probabilistic risk-taking and the courage to fail, making it more appropriate for those with the most experience.

The Right Environment

One of the most common questions we get from students who are highly competent but still frustrated in their inability to make change goes something like this: "How can I prompt change in my organization when its senior leadership resists it?" Our answer is an unsatisfying "You probably can't." No matter how capable you are, trying to make change within a structure or culture where it's not wanted is like swimming upstream. You might be able to do it for a while, but why? The progress is unlikely to stick, and everything will revert once you stop swimming.

Unfortunately, most entities' default response to change is resistance, even when they know they need it and have asked for it. Why? For the same reasons that humans react this way—the fear of threat or harm. They resist because trying something new is riskier than staying the same. Even problematic situations offer some level of stability and familiarity. People may be content with the status quo, even if it is dysfunctional, and prefer to regard their ways as traditional, classic, and unchangeable. They might reason that their values and views have served them well. They have succeeded until recently. Why should they risk changing when the outcome is unknown?

Resistance to a contemplated change may be due to a fear of unanticipated consequences that could alter the organization's culture or environment. The advocated change may fail to perform as needed or envisioned. The solution may create new problems worse than the original. The brand may be tarnished. Clients or customers may be angered. Employees may leave or partnerships may end. People may get fired. Resistance may also come from a different perception of the benefits of change. New technology may represent needed support to some and stressful retraining to others. What one group views as an improved process, another sees as unnecessary complexity. Power granted to one may be taken from another.

Structural Openness

Rather than fighting against organizations or situations that resist change, a better choice is to identify those entities that are at least somewhat open to the prospect. Each environment, community, or organization is distinct, and each has traditions and styles that govern the pace and nature of change within their confines. But certain practices and traits are more strongly associated with openness to change:

History of change: Evidence of past change is a reliable trait. Has the organization or the field evolved noticeably over the last decade? If so, has the change they've pursued been significant? Changing a logo or ad campaign is not as demanding as introducing a new source of revenue or instituting a new policy, but it could indicate a willingness to listen.

Data-driven decision-making: Basing decisions on facts and input also suggests an openness to change. Does the organization or the field regularly gather and examine input about its practices and beliefs? Do they pay attention to what they learn and make changes based on it? Viewing others' opinions and insights as a source of inspiration and guidance is a clear signal that an entity or an environment is open to change.

Organizational structure: The right structure is less about how flat the organization is and more about how cohesive, flexible, and interconnected it is. Is the structure tightly siloed where every business unit is self-contained and competes with every other business unit for resources and attention? Or does it have little to no structure, where decision-making seems random and no one really knows who's in charge of what? The ideal structure is somewhere in between, with enough agility, resilience, and adaptability to accept change but still have control.

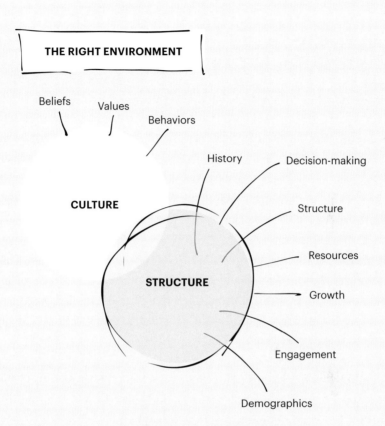

THE RIGHT ENVIRONMENT

Beliefs
Values
Behaviors
History
Decision-making
CULTURE
Structure
Resources
STRUCTURE
Growth
Engagement
Demographics

Finding the right environment

Resources: This one is tricky and nuanced, but worth examining. Where does the organization or environment get its inspiration and information? Are these resources entirely internal? If so, the community may be living in a bubble or controlling what they hear. If these resources are entirely external, coming from consultants or agencies, there may be insufficient knowledge and brainpower to pursue change. A mix of both is ideal.

Growth: This is another complex trait to interpret. Is the organization or environment growing or declining in relevance? Is its revenue base diverse or does it rely on a handful of large clients or donors? Growth sometimes indicates a willingness to change, but other times it represents leadership that is happy with the way things are. A decline can motivate a company to change, or it can be a symptom of an unwillingness to change. Look for the reason behind the numbers.

Engagement: Strong engagement is generally positive, but if leaders are micromanaging others, there's little openness to change. Are the organization's leaders and employees or volunteers aligned? Is there mutual trust and respect? Look for executive engagement that is empowering, not constraining.

Demographics: Younger people tend to be more open than older ones. Smaller organizations are usually more open than larger. Those with a diverse population tend to be more open than those with monocultures. Look closely at an organization's composition to get a sense of where they are on these spectrums.

These cautions aren't meant to restrict exploration. People try out different domains, particularly when they're young and searching to finding a better fit, but changemakers are wise to seek the most fertile ground possible because a resistant environment compounds the difficulty of making significant change, while an open one invites it, as Thomas Kelly, founder and CEO of Mexicue, clarified:

> *Over time, I realized the benefits of the company being open to change, and I became proactive about naming it as something that was important to our organization. We started talking about that being a part of our culture. It is something that is a strategic advantage of our business model: being open to changing our store, our format, our design within the stores, being able to go into different size stores, different existing restaurants.*

It doesn't matter that it's not a replica that we had done before. I started to see the advantages of embracing change in every way. Change is now a critical core part of our brand.

Cultural Flexibility

Further defining a community or organization's openness to change is its culture. Culture is an intangible asset that is revealed through the beliefs, values, and behaviors of its people. Even when it's not intentionally created or nurtured, it emerges from people's daily interactions, their response to new conditions, and their expectations of others. Whether cultural standards are documented or implied, they're most evident in what is rewarded. If a company rewards those who maintain tradition, declaring it's open to change is not convincing. If an organization says it encourages smart failure, but then punishes those who fail, believe the punishment.

Culture, whether in a company or at large, is the backdrop of any change project. It can act as a buoy, keeping a project afloat despite setbacks, or it can act as a lead weight, dragging a project to an early demise. An ideal cultural setting for change is one that is secure in its relevance and its role. It doesn't react to change as a threat requiring immediate resistance. Instead, it responds to it as an opportunity to review and test principles and established relationships. It represents the possibility of improvement or, if the change is not a good fit, the confirmation of existing values. A healthy culture sees its role as one of guidance, not intransigence, and makes room for dissent and questioning.

Just as an open culture allows change, a rigid culture shuts it down. It acts as an immune system and fights against any change as a threat. Cultures that react this way often have reasonable explanations for their inflexibility. They may resist potential modifications because they are highly respectful of their organization's history, traditions, and norms. Founders or leaders who initially developed the cultural principles may be revered, and the stock market may regularly reward them for using their habits and norms to deliver predictable returns. They may be charged with unifying a diverse population and be reluctant to risk the loss of cohesion, or they may be in a highly regulated industry without much room for variation.

Some cultures have been asked to accept "a new approach" so often and with such little benefit that they have no appetite for another serving. This happens regularly enough for it to have a name: change fatigue. People in these cultures have been repeatedly promised advantages that are never delivered. They don't necessarily express their resistance; instead, they offer the equivalent of a teen's eye roll and return to their normal tasks.

Bob Baxley
Veteran Design Leader

I worked at Apple for eight years and got really inculcated into that culture. Apple is a very aggressive, intense, honest culture. If you are part of that culture, you're totally fine with that. You can't have a fragile ego and survive in Steve Jobs's Apple.

When I went to Pinterest, they had posters on the conference walls that said, "Say the hard thing," as a reminder to people to say the hard thing. I can assure you, there was no poster in any conference room at Apple that said, "Say the hard thing." That's just how the company worked, and no one needed to be reminded.

So the big learning was that when people hire you because of your past experience from a notable company, they are hiring you for the values of that company, not the behaviors. I took all my Apple behaviors and tried to play them back at Pinterest, and it completely blew up in my face. This happened to tons of friends who made a similar transition.

What I've done with my new job—and my thoughts about what I've learned over time—is that I think hard about the values that the new company wants me to express. And then I think about how to express those values through behavior that the culture can accept. ▲

While some cultures' resistance to change is understandable, others are simply trying to protect the status quo without much thought as to whether that is the best course. They fear change will force them to reexamine their principles or guidelines, or it might introduce new com-plexities the organization prefers to ignore or suppress. Revising a cul-ture is a highly complex process that requires consensus among all levels of an organization and endorsement by its leadership. For some cultures, the risk of this happening as an outcome of a change initiative is too overwhelming.

Finding a fit by choosing the right problem in the right environment takes time and diligence, but without a productive pairing between a changemaker's competence and an organization's openness, any envi-sioned change will struggle to move forward. The ideal circumstance is obviously to find an open environment with a flexible culture that needs the capabilities and experience a changemaker can bring. Falling somewhat short of this ideal can still result in success, but likely with greater effort and more stress. Alternatively, a changemaker looking for the ultimate in both structural and cultural openness may be best served by joining a startup—the champions of change. Early stage startups can change their product, strategy, market, and more elements several times a year. As such, these companies are excellent training grounds for developing changemaker competence, experience, and leadership skills. You'll be following the founder's lead and working in chaotic, and often underfunded situations, but if you survive a few years, you could earn a black belt in changemaking.

Takeaways

Find a fit.
Changemakers who tackle problems truly suited to them leverage their competence, enhance their authority, and build their credibility.

Choose the right problem.
Those who lead change are asking others to follow them in a risky undertaking. While changemakers' competence is often broad and transferable to a range of problems, the ideal situation is where their abilities are core to solving the problem at hand and their experience is highly relevant.

Find an entity that's open to change.
Change is easy to request but hard to allow. Rather than fighting against organizations or institutions that resist change, a better choice is to find one that is at least open to the prospect.

Look for a culture that isn't too rigid.
Culture, whether in a company or at large, is the backdrop of any change project. It can act as a buoy, keeping a project afloat despite setbacks, or it can act as a lead weight, dragging a project to its early demise.

Take It Further

Culture Map: Breaking Through the
Invisible Boundaries of Global Business.
Erin Meyer. PublicAffairs, 2014.

Designing Your Life: How to Build a Well-Lived Joyful Life.
Bill Burnett and Dave Evans. Knopf, 2016.

Farnam Street Blog
(fs.blog)

"Life Advice That Doesn't Suck."
(markmanson.net/archive)

MakerMind
(nesslabs.com)

Master Class
(masterclass.com)

Mindset: The New Psychology of Success.
Carol S. Dweck, PhD. Random House, 2006.

The Genius Zone: The Breakthrough Process to
End Negative Thinking and Live in True Creativity.
Gay Hendricks and Sean Patrick Hopkins, et al.
St. Martin's Essentials, 2021.

Stanford Continuing Studies
(continuingstudies.stanford.edu)

Chapter 4

Foundations of Success

Making change is not cheap. Being in the right place with the right competence and appropriate authority allows a changemaker to make transformative change, but any significant project needs a strong foundation of support. That support comes from three pillars: a clear directive for change, a strong sponsor or champion with realistic and measurable expectations, and sufficient resources to execute.

Lacking any of this support creates imbalance. A well-designed and significantly backed directive to make change that doesn't have enough resources dedicated to it will underperform its potential, even with strong sponsorship. A wealth of resources applied against a directive that is vague or a sponsorship that is wavering will be rapidly wasted. A big budget and clear directive without a strong backer can be easily derailed. Each pillar needs to carry its portion of the weight for a change initiative to move from theory to practice.

How this support is delivered depends on the type and scale of change along with its context. If the setting is a large established organization—whether for profit or nonprofit, all aspects of gaining this support will be formal and likely to follow a multiphased approval process. A sizable undertaking could take one to two years to get finalized. If the setting is smaller and more bootstrapped, as with startups or new social movements, formal approval will be less important and decision-making faster, but support and resources may be much tougher to secure.

Clear Directive

The first pillar in the foundation for success is a clear, realistic directive that explains why change is needed. Whether phrased as a hypothesis or a conclusion, this directive makes it clear what needs to change, why it needs to change, what benefits should result, and what costs will be incurred and saved.

Similar to a creative brief, the directive provides a high-level summary of the initiative's goal and scope, but it may turn out to be wrong. It's rare that an original hypothesis of a problem remains unchanged throughout a project. As the team learns more about an organization, its processes, its context, and its stakeholders, the definition of the problem often shifts. For that reason, the directive is not meant to be a fixed definition, but rather a good faith attempt to identify what's wrong and why it needs to be addressed. It's an initial theory and set of assumptions that are subject to revision.

Sometimes the directive is well articulated at the start; other times it needs to be formulated or refined. Answering these five questions usually provides enough information:

Where is change needed? Detailing where change is needed should bound the project and clarify what is included and what isn't. The answer can be brief without extensive detail. For example, an organization's response could be "improve innovation practices" or "modernize the sales process." A political action committee answer could be "modify our approach to fundraising" or "improve outreach to supporters." A startup's goal could be "update how community members meet and interact" or "streamline our onboarding process." These descriptions aren't lengthy, but they are precise enough to indicate where the change needs to be made.

Why is the change needed now? Clarifying why the change is needed now is a simple way to determine the company's urgency to address it. It can also be a clue to how much thought and time they've put into the problem so far. If a startup is rushing to change how community members meet and interact because they want to show progress before a deadline for raising investment funds, the problem may be more a reaction to pressure than a real dilemma. Conversely, if their urgency stems from research showing that members are leaving the community because of interaction problems, that's a critical issue worth immediate attention.

CLEAR DIRECTIVE

Where is the change needed?

Why is the change needed now?

Which circumstances are prompting this change?

Who or what might resist the change?

What is the cost or consequence of not making this change?

A clear directive

Which circumstances are prompting this change? Similarly, learning which circumstances have prompted this desire for change can add dimension to its urgency. It can identify threats to the company or hint at potential benefits of success. For instance, does the political action committee want to revise its fundraising because it's growing rapidly or because it's taking on a new mission? Does the organization want to improve its innovation practices because new employees need asynchronous support or because the current approach is not producing acceptable results?

Who or what might resist this change? Speculating on the resistance this change might encounter is particularly valuable, even if it's a guess, because it provides a roadmap to possible landmines. Resistance could come from within. A political action committee wanting to revise how it connects with its supporters may meet resistance from those doing the outreach who may not want to take on more work. Or resistance could be external. An organization seeking to modernize its sales process may face resistance from clients or customers who like the current process. Resisters often have the power to slow or block any change. Identifying them early allows enough time to address their concerns.

What is the cost or consequence of not making this change? This question helps define the scope and timing of the project. If not making the change costs $10 million a year, then a project budget of $1 million seems cheap. If the cost of forgoing the change is less significant, the budget will be more constrained. As important, but more difficult to quantify, are consequences. For example, if the consequences of a startup *not* upgrading its onboarding process is that employees may be initially less productive, that's costly but hard to put a specific value on.

When finalized, the responses to these questions create a high-level overview of the problem or an opportunity that can guide and filter initial actions. Like an entrepreneur's elevator pitch, the summary should be concise, direct, and understandable—suggesting the key elements of the opportunity and staying above the particulars. But the most compelling directive is not worth the pixels it takes to communicate unless it's backed by a strong executive sponsor (or similar champion in a nonbusiness setting).

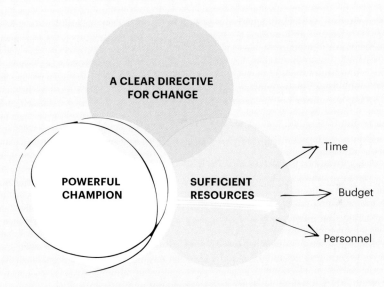

A CLEAR DIRECTIVE
FOR CHANGE

POWERFUL
CHAMPION

SUFFICIENT
RESOURCES

Time

Budget

Personnel

Foundations of success

Powerful Champion

Any significant change project requires backing from someone with power, influence, and the ability to secure resources. Within larger organizations, this person may be a senior executive able to authorize and fund a project and solicit the support and participation of others. In startups, it could be an investor capable of providing more funding. In nonprofits or community groups, it may be a major donor willing to underwrite the work.

Confirming a sponsor or champion starts with the question, "Who is asking for this change?" The answer should indicate who is willing to back the venture and provide cover to those working on it. If a change-maker responds, "I don't need backers because this is a grassroots vision," their ambition is admirable, but it's another example of swimming upstream. Sponsorship increases a stakeholder's agency and decreases the initiative's risk. It sustains the change effort during slow periods and protects it against detractors. It delivers resources. It gives weight to timelines, decisions, and requests, as Doug Powell, Vice President, Design Practice Management at Expedia, illustrated in this example from his time at IBM:

> *When you're impacting change in a mission, executive sponsorship is required. During my time at IBM, my boss Phil Gilbert had a dotted line to the CEO because he sat on her key Technical Advisory team. So, he had time on her agenda to come in and say, "Ginni, this is what's going on. Here's a couple of real wins, and here are a couple of areas that we're really falling on our faces." She listened, and we were able to use that access effectively. The business leaders and their units and divisions knew Phil had that access, so if Phil said, 'Hey, you guys are not performing on your NPS scores. What the fuck is going on?" They answered that call or that email because Phil had access to the CEO. I can't overstate how important that kind of access and support is.*

When a sponsor is championing an initiative, his or her opinion carries significant weight, but a single sponsor can also be a point of weakness. If this person leaves, the support may leave with them. A better choice is a network of sponsors, as many as three to four people who are all willing to back the venture. This approach may slow the decision-making because multiple sponsors often act like a board and need time to debate, but it provides more security. Any one person leaving is unlikely to sink the project.

Sometimes a sponsor is also the changemaker, such as when a founder or senior executive initiates a project. However, even if they can self-fund the project or have the authority to allocate money to it, they still need other champions or trusted advisors who can serve as sounding boards, offering feedback and counsel. They need peers who can provide insights and divergent perspectives and who can challenge assumptions. They need the respect and buy-in of other leaders to show that their idea has merit and is not a dictate.

Realistic Expectations

Both the change directive and the sponsor should reflect realistic expectations. Clearly articulated expectations help ensure that the project's parameters are understood, and that success is defined in a way that is achievable and demonstrable. In a typical design project, success is defined not in terms of the design itself, but rather its outcome. That outcome might be increased customer satisfaction or reduced complaints, improved perceptions, or stronger loyalty. It can be a compelling new concept that tests well in its intended market, a workable feature, or a better button. The definition of the project's success varies, depending on the assignment, but it's judged by its impact. The same should be true for change initiatives.

In this case, the question to ask is "If this project is successful, how will we know?" Reasonable answers are specific, achievable, and measurable. If the answer describes a relative improvement—a reversal of declining sales, greater outreach to voters, more community interaction—it may be sufficient. But the cleanest definition of success is a measure: a 5% increase in closed sales, 10 new viable ideas that can be developed over five years, or a community growth rate of 15% a year. This level of specificity, although sometimes difficult to define, makes a successful outcome more evident and helps clarify how to achieve it. This level of specificity from an executive sponsor or support ecosystem suggests the project has been thoughtfully considered and rationally scoped.

Unreasonable answers fall into three categories: vague or unaligned with the problem or opportunity, unattainable because of scope or demands, or unmeasurable. Saying "I can't tell you, but I'll know when I see it" is an extreme example of a vague response. Less extreme but still too hazy are responses like "Any improvement will be good," or "We'll become more cohesive." A better response would explain what measurable amount of improvement is considered "good" or what metric will indicate a community is more cohesive.

Reasonable definitions of success can be distorted by outsized scope or irrational expectations of time. Change will not solve all an organization's problems. It will not eliminate poor hires, weak quarters, or other normal business variations. It's unlikely to influence industry-wide trends. No amount of internal change could have prevented the demise of film development, movies on CDs, or pantyhose. Clear success criteria, such as "align all global design departments so they collaborate more smoothly," become unreasonable if it's expected to happen in a year.

Sufficient Resources

Realistic expectations and measures of success lead to an accurate estimate of the resources required to achieve that desired outcome. This is not the time to suggest you have supernatural powers to achieve the greatest success with the fewest resources. It's wiser to assume that the project will need more money, more time, and more people than you think. That's not an assumption of poor planning; rather it's the nature of change projects. Because they address complex problems, they routinely encounter unexpected developments and new challenges. Having sufficient resources anticipates these surprises and makes them less daunting.

If an organization or a sponsor asks for change, but doesn't resource it appropriately, that's a bright red flag that the change is not really supported. Each of these resource categories—time, budget, and personnel—is important and interrelated:

Time: Change projects take more time than initially estimated, but also can grow to fill whatever time is offered, so finding a balance is more of an agreement on what's reasonable than a commitment to a set duration. This agreement reflects the project's complexity and scale. How many other entities or decision-makers are involved? What approvals are required? How much research is needed? How many people need to be kept informed?

As a general rule of thumb subject to any number of caveats, smaller change projects can take one to two years while larger ones can take five or more years. Change projects will progress more slowly in

Sarah Brooks
Design Strategist, Practical Futurist

President Barack Obama created the Presidential Innovation Fellowship, uniting innovators and federal leaders to improve government for everyone. I had the honor of serving in the Fellows' 2014–2015 class at the V.A. Center for Innovation within the U.S. Department of Veterans Affairs, a complex organization of 400,000+ people. I learned powerful lessons in seizing the moment to gain senior-level support for a change mission in my first weeks on the job.

Amber Schleuning, then-leader of the V.A. Center for Innovation, had an opportunity to get in front of the new V.A. Secretary Bob McDonald as he was formulating his transformation strategy. Amber wanted data directly from Veterans on their wants and needs from the V.A., so her first directive to me was to design and lead a seven-person team on a research sprint across the country to talk with veterans and to then deliver the findings to Bob.

Amber had a can-do attitude and audacious goals to support her fellow veterans. She kept our team laser-focused and moving forward, knocking down the bureaucratic blockers. She was our champion. Bob saw the design approach as pivotal. He became Amber's champion, and with that, the work continued to develop and flourish. Bob created a coalition of change-makers across V.A. who worked up, down, and across the complexity of the organization to make service improvements that delivered better outcomes for veterans. Successes resulted from alignment on intent, a sense of urgency, creativity in addressing blockers, unwavering senior leader support, and an understanding of veterans' needs at the center. ▲

typically staid environments, like government and academia. They may move faster in unconstrained or spontaneous environments, like startups and urgent social movements. It's not uncommon for them to progress sporadically, moving quickly at times then slowing for a period. Regular reevaluations of the timeline and adjustments to reflect new conditions are smart actions to incorporate in any change process.

Budget: Change initiatives are costly. Most require a budget with at least five zeros and possibly one or two more, but at this point it's only an estimate. More detail and revision will be needed later. An early assessment can examine more strategic considerations; for example, the amount of direct costs, like personnel, travel, and supplies versus indirect costs, like administrative expenses. It can look at the ratio between fixed costs that remain stable throughout the project and variable costs that increase as the project scales. It can outline the need for setup costs versus operating expenses. More sophisticated approaches can include the consideration of opportunity costs (what the funds could finance if not directed toward the change project) or the cost of risk (such as what additional financial impact failure may have).

Ignoring costs or hoping they will be minimal inevitably slows the change process and can bring it to a halt. Surprising sponsors or stakeholders with unseen costs associated with changemaking can spur them to rethink the entire effort. As with most endeavors, it's safer to estimate higher expenditures than expected. No one will be disappointed if the final cost is lower than budgeted.

Personnel: Highly experienced, senior changemakers can often choose their own team, but most others can't. If working within an organization, a team may be assigned to a changemaker, and it may include people who do not report to him or her. In a nonprofit or community organization, a team will likely include volunteers who may or may not have the needed qualifications.

Any discussion of personnel should examine the trade-offs between outsourced help and internal workforces. Outsourced resources can provide more experienced professionals, greater speed and agility, and the benefit of being temporary. However, they are typically more expensive, time-consuming to find and select, and tougher to onboard and manage. Internal staff can be more dedicated to the project and more familiar with the environment, its processes, and its culture, but their true cost may be hidden. Change projects are almost always added burdens to an already full workload. Team members will need to juggle other priorities or work overtime. They also may be less expert on the topic and require time to learn new tools, techniques, or topics.

In most cases, diligently considering these foundations of success pays off. A clear directive, a strong sponsor with reasonable expectations, and sufficient resources provide a stable platform for the work to come, but even well-founded and properly funded change efforts encounter problems. They run into unexpected roadblocks, changed regulations, and random pandemics or wars. A key support person leaves the firm, or an unknown resistor shows up. Expectations change or a new, more pressing project saps resources. All of these disruptions and more can derail the best-laid plans, but with an open and supportive organization, a clearly defined problem or opportunity, realistic expectations, and sufficient resources, a change initiative has a fighting chance.

Takeaways

Ensure that you have support.

Any significant change project needs a strong foundation of support. That support comes from three pillars: a clear directive for change, a strong sponsor or champion with realistic and measurable expectations, and sufficient resources to execute.

Understand the goal.

Whether phrased as a hypothesis or a conclusion, a directive makes it clear what needs to change, why it needs to change, what benefits should result, and what costs will be incurred and saved.

Identify the sponsor and the expectations.

A change initiative requires backing from someone with power, influence, and the ability to secure resources. Clearly articulated expectations help ensure that the project's parameters are understood, and success is defined in a way that is achievable and demonstrable.

Confirm sufficient resources.

Realistic expectations and measures of success lead to an estimate of the resources required to achieve that desired outcome, most importantly, time, budget, and personnel.

Take It Further

Collective Illusions: Conformity, Complicity,
and the Science of Why We Make Bad Decisions.
Todd Rose. Hachette Go, 2022.

Forget a Mentor, Find a Sponsor:
The New Way to Fast-Track Your Career.
Sylvia Ann Hewlett. Harvard Business Review Press, 2013.

Harvard Business Review Project Management Handbook:
How to Launch, Lead, and Sponsor Successful Projects.
Antonio Nieto-Rodriguez. Harvard Business Review Press, 2021.

Start with Why: How Great Leaders
Inspire Everyone to Take Action.
Simon Sinek. Portfolio, 2011.

The First 90 Days: Proven Strategies for
Getting Up to Speed Faster and Smarter.
Michael D. Watkins. Harvard Business Review Press, 2013.

The Power of Crisis: How Three Threats—
and Our Response—Will Change the World.
Ian Bremmer. Simon & Schuster, 2022.

Chapter 5

Co-Creating Change

Change doesn't happen as the output of one person, no matter how enthusiastic or talented. Even wildly famous visionaries, like Steve Jobs or Martin Luther King, couldn't have achieved their goals without a team of people who believed in their ideas and worked together to make them real. People who shared the same purpose and passion but may not have had the confidence, capacity, or vision to pull it all together. Building alliances with these people and inviting them to join forces and contribute what they can scale the ability to make change.

Whether leading a movement, reviving an organization, or starting a new venture, a changemaker needs to attract and align a team willing to work together in a highly ambiguous context with more questions than answers. That happens more readily when a change project's intentions are earnest and clear, and where contributors' efforts are needed and valued. Contributors gravitate toward changemakers who can establish a sense of shared purpose, without diminishing individual expertise and perspective. They admire leaders who can communicate inspiring visions that remain open to modification. They stick with leaders who allow pivots and new approaches without losing momentum, and who are able to preserve support through inevitable downturns.

Becoming this type of leader requires a humble, yet impactful, approach to influence, built on a realistic appreciation of the challenges of making collective change without dominating. It relies on a willingness to deploy strengths and offset weaknesses, along with the patience to bridge differences and link diversity. It depends on healthy relationships and safe, productive environments where egos are controlled and spotlights are shared. This style of leadership can be inherent, or it can be learned. When faulty, members disengage. When it's sound, magic happens.

The Good and the Bad

Co-creation has risen in prominence because it produces better outcomes. People are smarter and more creative collectively than they are individually. Partly this is simple math: each brain contributes more capability, and more is better than less. Additionally, multiple brains operating in harmony work more efficiently than loosely aligned work groups. These are significant advantages, and if the collaborating brains also think differently or are influenced by different experiences, combining them is even more beneficial.

Diversely populated groups produce more original ideas. Different avenues are explored, and more options uncovered. In addition to pumping up a team's creative and perceptive abilities, diversity reduces bias. Collaborations with mixed perspectives make predispositions more apparent and force more discussion and debate. When in support of a shared goal, these discussions improve clarity and meaning and lead to a better solution. Granted, constant discussion and debate can be stifling, but once members understand each other's strengths and weaknesses and trust each other's intent, co-creation teams can work through their differences quickly and effectively.

Another valuable aspect of co-creation is its ability to leverage individual strengths for the collective benefit. For example, when experienced pros collaborate with fresh-thinking novices in creating change, the chance of its successful adoption increases. The novices can contribute inventiveness and ambitions unburdened by past experience, but the experienced pros know how to execute and gain support.

Because of these benefits, it's smart to define group diversity beyond ethnic or cultural differences. There is value in bringing together people with different income or educational levels, different functional expertise, and different methods of reasoning or intuitive approaches. Diverse viewpoints can come from all flavors of gender identification and sexual orientation, extraverts and introverts, the wildly experimental and the steadfastly traditional. Tall people and short people experience the world differently, as do younger and older people. The physically disabled go through life differently, as do those on the spectrum. Each of these perspectives can add greater breadth and dimension to explorations and the search for workable solutions.

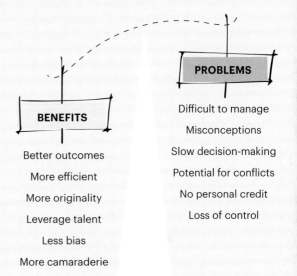

BENEFITS

Better outcomes

More efficient

More originality

Leverage talent

Less bias

More camaraderie

PROBLEMS

Difficult to manage

Misconceptions

Slow decision-making

Potential for conflicts

No personal credit

Loss of control

The balancing act of co-creation

Individual Benefits

The heightened level of connection and cooperation required to co-create doesn't mean members are anonymous drones. Belonging to a co-creative change effort affords personal as well as team advantages. Membership adds to identity and reaffirms values, but people can also learn from those with different skills, responsibilities, world views, or lived experience. This broadened perspective raises compassion and empathy, but also improves a person's ability to advocate for a specific viewpoint—not to dominate, but to share an alternative opinion and hopefully influence the discussion.

Learning to co-create and collaborate effectively decreases the urge to compete with others and makes it easier to negotiate. Instead of approaching a situation with an "us versus them" attitude, changemakers working in concert can rely on relationships and mutual respect. The objective becomes one of sharing strengths, compensating for weaknesses, and pursuing common desires, with the recognition that although everyone may think and perform differently, all can contribute. Christina Wodtke, Stanford University lecturer, illustrated how these benefits showed up in her day-to-day team interactions:

> *When I first started managing at Yahoo, my team sat together. One of my designers just hated her PM. The PM was coming over every five minutes. "How's it going? Is it working? Do you need anything for me? Can I do something?" She would hide from this PM because he drove her crazy. Then we re-orged and she had to sit next to her enemy. About two weeks later, she comes over to me and goes, "Oh my god, my poor PM—people are yelling at her all day long." She started feeling empathy for the PM, and they ended up working together to figure out how to solve the stresses from above. There is a lot of power in realizing that the enemies are the competitor and not the person sitting next to you.*

Hurdles and Headaches

Despite the group and individual benefits, effective co-creations are difficult to sustain. They often suffer from a combination of fine intentions and sufficient talent, but poor execution. The goal is often miscast as reaching consensus, so people fear their efforts will be unacknowledged or diminished to suit others. They worry that everything will require group input and will move too slowly. Or that conflict is inevitable and arguments will abound. Or that roles and responsibilities will be only vaguely defined and that goals will fluctuate with stock prices or an executive's bonus structure.

Even when co-creation teams have the right attitudes and abilities, the dynamics of truly working together are formidable. If a change initiative is run by a selfish leader with little to no empathy for others, it can discourage input and encourage half-hearted work. If the lead is overly status conscious or clinging to power, the team will sense that attitude and avoid questioning any decision. If the leader doesn't spend sufficient time clarifying commitments and responsibilities, efforts will overlap, be redundant, or be disproportionately shared. Even leaders who strive to be inclusive can introduce bias unknowingly, triggering discomfort and fear.

Any of these conditions or concerns would be problematic in a straightforward collaboration. When the intent is co-creating change, they directly interfere with the fluid teamwork needed for success. It's like saying, "let's design a circumstance where everyone fears the most discomfort possible with the least satisfaction imaginable." As a result, people often see a changemaking venture as something to avoid—an aspirational ideal that is destined to devolve into a brawling power grab.

Forge Fluidity

What transforms a tumble of semi-willing participants into a streamlined engine of innovative and effective changemaking is appropriate and effective leadership. Not the outdated command-and-control approach or even more recent styles relying on charisma or bravado, but an approach to leadership that depends on partnering—on an acknowledgment and acceptance of shared contribution and responsibility.

Partnering doesn't diminish a leader's role or impact. There is distinct and important value in a change leader's ability to architect the way forward, to see and explain an outcome that may not yet be evident to others. There's value in building connections that amplify benefits and minimize harm. A leader is needed to make hard decisions when consensus is not possible. These capabilities drive momentum, maintain support, and make the potential for change real, but only if a change leader is fully enmeshed in a competent, cohesive, and adaptable team.

Whether team members have been hand-picked, assigned, or volunteered, their ability to work together has profound influence on a change project. A process that goes through many stages needs team members who are willing to shift roles, responsibilities, and power. It needs team members with different abilities and creative styles who can accept that they are better suited to certain phases than to others. It greatly benefits from trust, respect, and a deep level of bonding. A changemaker facilitates this flexibility and initiates this connection not only by uncovering teammates' strengths and weaknesses, but also by discerning their hopes and fears, their values and expectations.

Determine Substance and Style

Just as changemakers need to understand and acknowledge their own individual strengths and weaknesses, so too must they understand their team's abilities and gaps. Teams with a clear and accurate understanding of each other's capabilities can better allocate their strengths and compensate for their weaknesses.

Team members are typically evaluated on functional talents, but co-creation assessments include more dimension and greater depth. A candid review of strengths and weaknesses can start with skills and then shift to beliefs, behaviors, and preferences. How do they relate to others? Are they engaged and inspired by the project's potential or only following orders? Are they likely to generate creative contributions or raise challenges, push the group to think deeply about their assumptions, or to double-check assessments? Without insights like these, team relationships are functional at best and unlikely to hold up in the face of inevitable challenges.

Changemakers can encourage this level of honesty and transparency by being authentic and vulnerable—by sharing their own concerns, their own weaknesses, and their own struggles. They can role model how to ask for support when needed. They can emphasize that seeking help is not a weakness, but a recognition of another's value. Rather than frightening teammates or creating insecurity, this type of openness often generates the same in return.

Another aspect of a team's collective strengths and weaknesses is how their individual collaboration styles mesh. Collaboration styles are the behaviors and attitudes that people use when working together to reach a shared goal or objective. They are default patterns developed over time that are difficult to modify. If you task your favorite search engine for a list of these styles, it will happily respond with dozens of choices. We don't have the omnipotence of search algorithms, but we've each led hundreds of co-creations and worked with a wide range of collaborators. These are the most common styles we've seen used by leaders or contributors.

The Director: Directors like to set goals and direct the team's progress, even if they are not officially in charge. They are comfortable making decisions without too much input and are able to provide clear direction to others. They prefer focusing on execution, ideally with a detailed plan as a guide. Given their authoritative style, they are likely to be less flexible and less creative. If they try to micromanage others, they demoralize the team and erode motivation.

The Creative: Creatives like to expand outlooks and ideas. They are comfortable taking risks and are open to diverse perspectives. They stay relatively flexible and extend that flexibility to others, welcoming others' input. They often have a visual orientation that can be a unique asset, but their effusive nature can make them seem disorganized and undisciplined. If they can't shift from ideation to implementation, they disrupt progress.

The Team Player: Team players are the personification of group democracy, striving for harmony and inclusivity. They set the stage, explain the context to newcomers, and clarify any confusions. They seek input from everyone. Their main weakness is an insensitivity to time and deadlines. They can allow overanalysis and too much debate.

The Project Manager: Project managers are goal-driven and highly organized, setting the team's pace and ensuring the timely completion of tasks. They have a keen sense of others' strengths and weaknesses and seek to keep everyone aligned and working together. The flip side of their strengths are their weaknesses. Their focus on progress can leave insufficient time or attention for content. Their superhuman discipline and drive can burn others to a crisp.

The Challenger: Challengers look for holes or gaps in arguments or ideas. They play devil's advocate, always searching for alternatives and downsides. They push for closer scrutiny, slowing a team's pace and increasing deliberation. Their diligence is rewarded when hidden problems and flaws are identified, but their resistance can be alienating, drain the team's energy, and erode trust.

The Coach: Coaches help others do their best work by cheering them on, thanking them regularly, and inspiring them to reach higher. They recognize the value of diverse skill sets and reserve judgment of others. They are a keen developer of talent but have a hard time staying on task. They may lose sight of the goal, focusing disproportionately on the people trying to achieve it.

Any of these styles can be effective. The challenge is their integration. Guiding how best to meld the benefits and drawbacks of each is one of the roles of a team charter.

A Team Charter

A team charter blends members' capabilities and styles into a shared identity that holds it together despite different roles and responsibilities. A charter sets a team's intentions by stating its overall goal and key objectives, defining roles and relationships, highlighting shared values, and anticipating potential struggles—all in support of smoothing collaboration among members.

The details and extent of a team charter differ from one instance to another, but if it covers these categories, it will help reduce confusion, confirm acceptable conduct, and delineate accountability.

Overall goal and supporting objective: The overall goal and objectives uniting the team are essentially the change directive that is backed by a champion or sponsor. It may include more details of relevance to the team, or it may be the original now shared with the team.

Shared values: Shared team values are principles that encourage mutual respect and empathy. Instead of leaving responses up to human nature or personality traits, shared values guide members on how to react when their ideas are dismissed or their abilities doubted. They recognize that multiple viewpoints are available and clarify how team members should interact with each other in settings that might provoke anger or frustration. They encourage accepting differences, looking for similarities, and making sense of contradictions. Minor disagreements may abound, but shared values can keep them from growing into major conflicts.

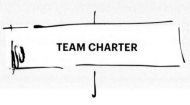

TEAM MEMBERS
Who is on our team and what is each person's strengths, weaknesses, and role?

GOALS AND SUPPORTING OBJECTIVES
What are we trying to achieve?

SHARED VALUES
What values do we want to honor while working together?

RISKS, ISSUES, OR OBSTACLES
What might prevent us from achieving our goals? What ways can we mitigate these risks?

Team Charter

Risks, issues, or obstacles: Defining risks, issues, or obstacles that might challenge the team is a simple way of alerting members to potential struggles and making it clear that these won't be surprises or failings. Topics might include what is in scope and what is not, where resistance might lie, what potential market forces or regulatory limitations could complicate the process, and any other potential challenges.

A charter can't direct every type of behavior or interaction, but it can indicate what is desired. When well-designed and appreciated by all team members, it helps establish a working environment that is psychologically and creatively safe. This type of environment—one that is encouraging and protective—not only improves a team's performance, but also accords them the respect and recognition they deserve, as Janice Fraser, author of *Farther, Faster, and Far Less Drama*, urged:

If we don't make it safe to try, then the people who try—who actually are very heroic because they're putting all sorts of things at risk by trying a new thing—they will go away or they will be punished. We need to make it possible for folks to opt into these new mindsets and behaviors. So that commitment to creating safe conditions is really an important theme.

A Safe Environment

A safe environment sets predictable and reasonable standards. Responsibilities and workloads are appropriately assigned. Plans are intelligible. Timelines are tolerable. Guidelines are not overly tolerant or mindlessly pleasant, but rather they promote conditions and attitudes that strengthen people's productivity, participation, and satisfaction. Safe environments encourage members to freely give and accept help. They clarify that everyone will be judged on what is accomplished together, but that those accomplishments are made up of individual contributions. They also make clear what is not supportive, such as being territorial, hoarding information, taking credit for another's work, or talking over quieter members.

These environments reward authenticity and normalize vulnerability. No one is attacked or demeaned. Dissenting voices and different points of view are treated as legitimate and worth considering. Opinions are allowed to change in the light of new information. Care is taken to help team members feel a sense of agency—to feel seen and appreciated for their efforts.

This is not just a "feel good" exercise. Safe environments heighten creativity. Safe environments support experimentation and smart risk-taking. When members trust they won't be punished for small failures, they are better able to grow and learn from them.

Another benefit of establishing a safe environment is that it fortifies connection and agility among members, particularly when desired behaviors are role-modeled and reinforced by a leader. An effective leader makes it clear that a team's success depends on relationship building, and that cooperation must be consensual and unforced, as Catherine Courage, VP of Google Consumer UX, noted:

> *So much of effective collaboration is about face time and building relationships with people and building trust. You can't just swoop in. Even though you may know exactly how the problem needs to be solved and what needs to happen, it never works when you dominate. Take the time and build the relationships with folks—otherwise, you just won't be successful.*

Team relationships grow over time and through challenges. Some will be closer than others, but all should have a basis in mutual respect and trust. But teamwork can hide singular contributions or mash them up into an undifferentiated group effort. Effective leaders counter this when it's evident they care about teammates—about their ideas, their contributions, and their well-being—in ways that recognize them as individuals and convey a sense of trust. Simple actions like voicing frequent "thank-yous" and celebrating small gains lets teammates know they're seen and acknowledged.

An even more significant action is sharing power. Good co-creative leaders understand how and when to strengthen relationships by letting others lead, perhaps because a colleague's talents are better suited to an assignment or to build a more cohesive bond with group members. That's not to say this is easy. Holding power becomes familiar and comfortable. Handing it off to another person feels risky. But taking that chance visibly demonstrates and builds trust. It also trains others to lead, increasing their value to the team.

A safe environment doesn't eliminate accountability. If anything, it demands more of it. A leader who doesn't hold others responsible for their commitments can risk damaging relationships with those who have to pick up the slack. Members who demand too much attention or consideration risk overshadowing the goal and objectives of making change. If expectations are clearly spelled out in the beginning, accountability is a matter of follow-through and consistency—actions that contribute to even greater psychological safety.

A co-creative team with a passionate and purposeful leader can overcome formidable odds. A diverse, fluid collaboration guided by a clear charter and sustained by a safe environment produces well above-average outcomes. This may not eliminate heated debate or dissent, or misunderstandings and flawed interactions. But by building mutual trust, encouraging honest and open communication,

Justin Maguire III
Chief Design Officer of Salesforce

I just want to be collaborative by nature. This myth of the heroic lone designer with their turtleneck and sketch book, solving world problems by themselves in the corner—I just never believed in it. Our job collectively is to bring great ideas and solutions out to customers. It doesn't matter if it's the janitor's idea.

I get close to people and start with, "Well, my worldview is this: What's yours? Take me on a harbor tour of your brain and how you think about customers." It's so disarming, and it hands power to them in many ways. It invites conversation.

In many companies, like here at Salesforce for instance, there are many GMs. There are many heads of development. There's one of me, and there's many marketing people, and there's many salespeople. And so in their world, many of them view success as a zero sum game, that they win at someone else's expense. I'm not a threat to anybody. When I do well, they all do well. ▲

and by rewarding the willingness to act in unison, a team can take on organizational transformation with confidence and agility—not as a top-down directive, but as a co-creative journey with a cohort of like-minded changemakers.

Takeaways

Change takes a team.
Change doesn't happen as the output of one person. It takes a team of people who believe in their ideas and work together to make them real. Building alliances with these people and inviting them to join forces scale the ability to make change and increase its chance of success.

Co-creating with others is hard.
Co-creation has risen in prominence because it produces better outcomes, but even when teams have the right attitudes and abilities, the practice of truly working together is formidable.

Lead as a partner.
What transforms a tumble of semi-willing participants into a streamlined engine of innovative and effective changemaking is appropriate and effective leadership. It's not the outdated command-and-control approach or even more recent styles relying on charisma or bravado, but an approach to leadership that depends on partnering—on an acknowledgment and acceptance of shared contribution and responsibility.

Build fluidity.
Teams with a clear and accurate understanding of each other's capabilities can better allocate their strengths and compensate for their weaknesses. Team charters can blend members' capabilities and styles into a shared identity that holds it together despite different roles and responsibilities. Relationships can be built, and safe environments created.

Take It Further

A Culture of Safety: Building a Work Environment Where People Can Think, Collaborate, and Innovate.
Alla Weinberg. Spoke & Wheel, 2020.

Group Genius: The Creative Power of Collaboration.
Keith Sawyer. Basic Books, 2006.

Leading with Emotional Courage: How to Have Hard Conversations, Create Accountability, and Inspire Action on Your Most Important Work.
Peter Bergman. Wiley, 2018.

Shifting the Monkey: The Art of Protecting Good People from Liars, Criers, and Other Slackers.
Todd Whitaker. Solution Tree, 2014.

The Culture Code: The Secrets of Highly Successful Groups.
Daniel Coyle. Bantam, 2018.

The Five Dysfunctions of a Team: A Leadership Fable.
Patrick Lencioni. Jossey-Bass, 2002.

The Power of Giving Away Power: How the Best Leaders Learn to Let Go.
Matthew Barzun. Optimism Press, 2021.

Chapter 6

Following a Map

Even the most experienced changemakers can get lost without a map. Typically, the map is an agreed-upon process—a series of actions completed in a predetermined order that leads to an envisioned outcome. Choosing and implementing the right process can be the difference between drifting or erratic progress and deliberate, steady advancement. Ironically, many people associate processes with stern rules and inflexible boundaries that inhibit free-flowing creativity, but adopting a basic procedure for working together allows a team to be both more creative and productive. Putting effort into choosing an appropriate process to follow rewards everyone involved.

The right operating process silently moves action along, giving members a sense of control while allowing exploration of novel ideas or implementations. By defining the project's path—what needs to be accomplished for what reasons and in what order—the team's collective brain power is channeled toward creative effort, rather than logistics. By suggesting the project's pace and noting key milestones, a process helps establish a shared sense of momentum and advancement. A solid process with mutually accepted rules, frameworks, and tools aligns team efforts and removes unnecessary friction. Most importantly, a well-designed operating process unites collaboration from start to finish by connecting a wide range of activities and showing their interdependence. Kevin Bethune,

Founder and Chief Creative Officer of dreams · design + life, put its value in perspective:

> *A creative journey is a myriad of guideposts, and you've got to know your situation and context in order to pick the right guideposts and use the right tool. If you're truly serving your team and not just feeding into your own power and privilege, are you giving them the right enablers so that they understand what their job is and what success looks like?*

Choosing the right process influences how the team works together. If a process is too onerous, it can deflate team members' enthusiasm and sap their creative abilities. Processes with too much structure, too much documentation, and too much tracking can dominate a project, slowing progress to a crawl. Conforming to the dictates of the process becomes the objective. If a process is too loose, team members can interpret its requirements differently. They can employ different tools or methods than other members. "Workarounds" can arise without documentation or explanation. Under time pressure, steps may be eliminated or dramatically shortened without a discussion of what is being lost.

Choosing the Right Process

Getting teams to accept a process is usually not hard. It's the rare project team that undertakes a challenge without some level of organization and structure, even if it's cursory. The struggle is determining which process to adopt. There are a multitude of choices available and more developed each year. Every industry has at least two or three standard processes, and large organizations often invent or refine their own versions. Individuals may differ in their process preference and push for adoption of one that is familiar to them. The choice is highly dependent on the setting, the goal, and the team, but it benefits from knowledge of the options available.

Several popular operating process options are currently in circulation, and each has its strengths and weaknesses.

Waterfall: The Waterfall process divides a project into discrete phases that happen in a mostly linear and sequential manner. Each phase is completed by those with expertise specific to that phase and then they "hand off" the project to the next team. This process is typical in industries and environments where changes can't be easily iterated, where development flows mainly in one direction from conception to deployment (such as construction and manufacturing), or where there are many stakeholders and a formal approval process.

Waterfall is favored for its predictable progress and its clear definitions of responsibility, but it doesn't allow for much variation after the start. It's also subject to disruption or delay if a group misses their deadlines. Mistakes are costly, so oversight tends to be more strict and rigid.

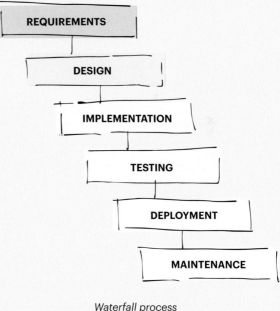

Waterfall process

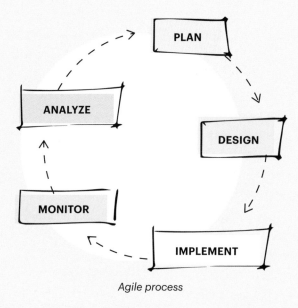

Agile process

Agile: The Agile process is more collaborative and interactive than the Waterfall approach. It provides a framework where self-organizing and cross-functional teams can work simultaneously. Rather than strictly defined handoffs and linear progression, Agile promotes adaptive planning, iterative development, and continual improvement using "scrums" and other techniques to coordinate group actions. Although it was started as a way to develop software, it has expanded into other industries as well.

Agile is favored for its flexibility and resilience. Problems can be addressed almost anywhere in the process, and no group necessarily depends on another. However, it is complex to execute properly and almost cultish in its emphasis on unique rituals and terms. Agile started as a pure development process, which has made it difficult to weave in traditional design processes, like big picture strategic thinking and up-front research that may not fit nicely into a sprint cycle. It requires

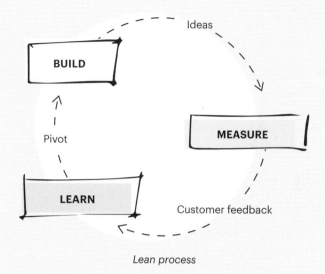

Lean process

flexibility and adaptability to incorporate those elements into the process. Without experienced guidance, it can easily spiral into chaos.

Lean: The Lean Startup approach is more a philosophy than a process but has notable elements. It aims to shorten development cycles by rapidly discovering if potential customers value the key features of a product, service, or experience. Lean does this through hypothesis-driven experimentation, iterative "beta" releases, and "pivots" driven by learnings. It is most common among startups and small companies that feel pressured to get to market quickly and who aren't punished for early missteps.

Lean is favored for its elevation of user feedback, its speed, low cost, and inherent flexibility. It's not applicable to all fields (for example, it's tough to develop a car, a theme park, or an immersive experience using Lean), and it can deliver wildly inaccurate guidance if poorly managed or implemented.

Design Processes

Designers work within all the previously described processes and more, depending on their environment and the task. When designers are working for an organization, a process may be mandated, but if they can choose their own, there are alternatives specifically intended for design projects.

In the "less structure is more" camp are processes that promote undirected exploration and brainstorming, followed by an inspiration that narrows and defines the outcome. Similar loose processes emphasize an iterative process of development and feedback with little exploration beyond what is directed by the feedback. These processes can work for one-person teams but are very difficult to scale. Because they are vague and conceptual, they can be stretched and reconfigured to suit a wide range of projects, but their informal, equivocal approach makes them an unrealistic choice for making significant change.

A more structured design-oriented processes is the Double Diamond model. Popularized by the British Design Council in 2005, it's a divergence-convergence model with four defined stages, all conveniently starting with the letter D: Discover, Define, Develop, and Deliver.

The first stage, Discover, encourages a broad and deep understanding of what is desired, what companies can offer, and what marketplaces can support. This stage is exploratory but within constraints of time, budget, and overall objective.

The Define stage narrows the project focus and determines areas of development or direction. This stage is reductive, filtering all that is learned in the Discover stage and identifying a way forward that is feasible, viable, and a fit with what customers want or need. The third stage, Develop, creates solutions appropriate to the areas defined in the previous stage,

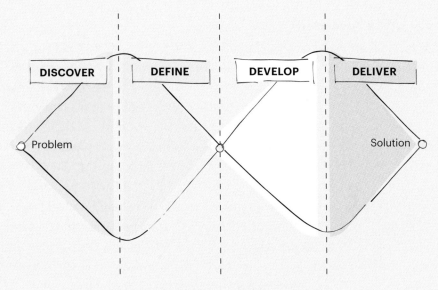

Double Diamond process

incorporating some iteration, but with an emphasis on producing concepts or prototypes that others can review. The final Deliver stage ideally results in a well-designed solution to the originally identified problem or opportunity.

Double Diamond is a solid process that has contributed to countless new products, services, and experiences. Its emphasis on customer and stakeholder input provides a solid foundation for eventual market success. Its reliance on visual expression and inclusive collaboration enhances creative output. And its appreciation for iteration—trial and error—promotes refinement and fit.

Like all processes, the Double Diamond has its shortcomings, particularly if applied to solving complex problems and dealing with resistant stakeholders. Unless its phases are viewed as recursive, it suggests a linear approach to problem-solving that is unrealistic and unlikely. A team could spend a decade thinking expansively about a complex problem and never find the root of it. The true cause might not be discovered until iterating in the development stage. Or it might not fully show up until the solution is delivered and the problem mutates into a new form. Likewise, there's no reason a team can't be discovering and defining in tandem. Or defining and developing as a feedback loop. Phases can and do happen simultaneously.

Also, just as Lean was developed for startups and Agile for software, Double Diamond was developed for creating or redesigning a single solution, expressed as a product, service, or experience. Changemakers may be exploring and evaluating multiple solutions simultaneously, with interactive ramifications. Their solution may end up being a product, a service, and an experience or more, all rolled into one.

Modified for Making Change

For most change projects, the Double Diamond approach works well, both conceptually and directionally, but in our experience, it benefits from a few modifications that deal with the shortcomings noted.

Discover: This first phase needs a reasonable balance between exploration and constraint. Too much exploration and the team wastes time, money, and effort on areas that prove unfruitful. Too much constraint and the team may miss important information or inspiration. This can only be accomplished if this stage is left "open," allowing the team to return to it as they gain new information or learn new options. This phase also needs early and active involvement of stakeholders. They can contribute significant assets, experience, and cautions that will inform the team and improve their productivity. The modification we advocate is to treat stakeholders as customers, similar to the Lean process, getting their input on ideas and experiments early and often.

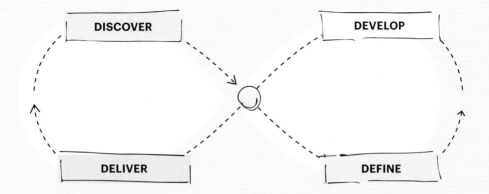

Double Diamond process modified for change

Define: This phase needs to offer a vision of the desired outcome and guidance on how to achieve it. We've found that it benefits from overlapping with the Discover stage, as a new discovery can lead to a new vision and vice versa. This phase also sets priorities and lays out areas for experimentation and prototyping. As with the Discover stage, stakeholder involvement is required.

Develop: For a change initiative, this is an iterative stage that tests out hypotheses, reviews results, and tries again until successful. It can overlap with the Define stage, providing feedback on what's working and what's not. It benefits from incorporating aspects of the Agile process, particularly those that coordinate simultaneous experimentation and development.

Deliver: This stage is less about a single solution and more about slowly and carefully scaling successful experiments and monitoring them to ensure appropriate impact and results. With changemaking, this stage almost always circles back to Discover as new problems or opportunities show up, making it more cyclical than linear.

With these modifications, the Double Diamond approach provides the fluidity and iteration a change initiative demands. It outlines the order of phases and frames their general intent, but makes clear the importance of stakeholder participation and iterative development. It guides experimentation, allowing for inventiveness and learning, and it recognizes the need for a slow, deliberate scaling of solutions.

Rules of Engagement

All processes, no matter how thoughtful and apt, are just drawings until they are put into practice. To work as intended, a process needs to be well understood by all team members and appropriately extended into plans and frameworks. It needs to be steered by shared operating agreements that delineate progress, select tools and platforms, define expectations for participation and communication, and specify how conflict is resolved. Clarifying and documenting each of these components up front save countless hours that would be lost in confusion and frustration. They serve as "pre-mortems" as design strategist Sarah Brooks noted, outlining what the team wants to happen in the future.

> *I believe producing shared agreements at the beginning of a project is essential in creating healthy conditions for a team to do their best work. This includes getting all team members' hopes and fears on the table, then negotiating agreements on how we will work together regarding roles, processes, tools, cadences, feedback loops, and resolving disagreements. I'm grateful to have learned this durable practice at Hot Studio in 2005.*

The required level of detail varies by project size, complexity, and member preferences. Larger projects with more stakeholders and rigid decision-making processes tend to need more steps and more time. Smaller projects can get by with less, but at a minimum, the team should agree on specific project objectives and plans, roles and responsibilities, and ground rules for working together.

Objectives and Plans

Project objectives break down the change directive into achievable assignments or deliverables. They're further detailed by plans that indicate how the process will proceed. They can be expressed as statements or formalized as team OKRs (Objectives and Key Results) or KPIs (Key Performance Indicators) or any other relevant metric that the team agrees to observe.

Objectives clarify specific outcomes. If the change directive is to improve an organization's innovation practices, the objective would indicate how that might happen. For example, the objective might be to explore existing internal and competitive innovation practices and define potential solutions that can be prototyped and tested prior to full implementation. If a change directive is to improve outreach to supporters, the objective might be to engage supporters in discussion and development of alternative means of outreach. Objectives don't need to be lengthy explanations, but they need to indicate the approach that the team will take to achieve their goal and what success will look like.

Objectives become more concrete when translated into a plan or timeline. Timelines are high-level renderings of the interdependent and chronological actions that will lead up to a solution. They indicate where a team is in the process they're following. If properly designed, they reveal how each action connects to the whole and how a slowdown in one area impacts other areas. Timelines can be based on estimates, but major milestones should be identified with time divided among them. When properly designed and maintained, timelines serve as excellent

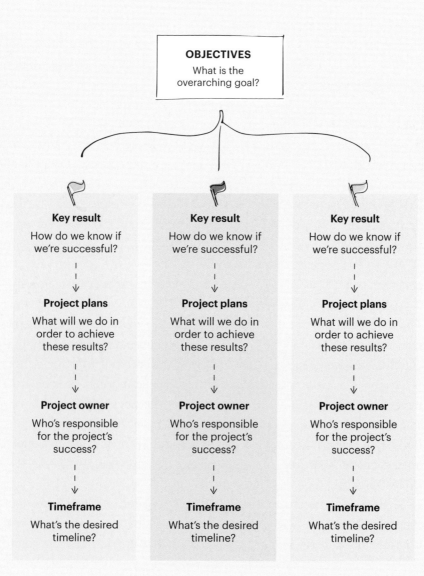

OBJECTIVES
What is the
overarching goal?

Key result	Key result	Key result
How do we know if we're successful?	How do we know if we're successful?	How do we know if we're successful?
Project plans	Project plans	Project plans
What will we do in order to achieve these results?	What will we do in order to achieve these results?	What will we do in order to achieve these results?
Project owner	Project owner	Project owner
Who's responsible for the project's success?	Who's responsible for the project's success?	Who's responsible for the project's success?
Timeframe	Timeframe	Timeframe
What's the desired timeline?	What's the desired timeline?	What's the desired timeline?

Objectives and plans

backdrops for process decisions because they are unemotional representations of what is happening.

Plans and timelines need some level of flexibility to survive the surprises and detours a change initiative often encounters. But this level of flexibility shouldn't be left to chance. It should be an agreement the team accepts. Without a specific agreement, flexibility may mean "whenever possible" to some and "a day or two past the stated deadline" to others.

Roles and Responsibilities

Assigning roles and responsibilities is like choosing players for a sports team. You want the strongest collection of skills possible, but each player needs to be relevant to the position. If you have three excellent pitchers and no catcher, you're not going to win many games. Your first goal is to make sure that you have the needed team members and that their skills are appropriate to the tasks. The accompanying goal is to clarify who does what. Again, if everyone wants to pitch and no one is willing to catch, the team suffers.

Beyond detailing the functional definition of who does what, it helps to also clarify relational responsibilities. Using a framework like DACI (Driver, Approver, Consulted, Informed) or RACI (Responsible, Accountable, Consulted, Informed) streamlines this task by identifying who drives forward progress, who has authority to approve decisions, who needs to be consulted, and who needs to be informed. Used appropriately, these frameworks can help prevent overassigning any one team member or inadvertently setting up conflicting roles.

Although teams typically have only one or two leaders, it's possible and beneficial to let people lead when their strength is most needed. If brainstorming is not a leader's strength, then someone else can lead the session. The most financially astute team member can lead a budget discussion and the most organized person can lead a planning session. This is an efficient and effective approach to teamwork. Done well, it doesn't detract or dilute the group leader's role.

The final action is to hold people accountable for meeting their responsibilities. Categorizing excuses helps identify patterns. For example, if most missed deadlines or incomplete tasks are the result of influences beyond a team member's control, it could indicate that the initiative does not have enough executive support. If a team member fails to accomplish their goals due to their own actions, it could indicate they are not a good fit for the project.

Ground Rules

Ground rules are agreements that guide day-to-day progress and interactions. They relate to the high-level guidance of a team charter, but are more specific to the project and its objectives. They might include whether meetings happen in person or via conferencing, how asynchronous interactions are coordinated, what common tools the team will use, or what templates they'll employ. They emerge from a group discussion and shared decision-making and are highly subjective, but here are some favorites.

Progress check-ins: Team members need to be accountable for completing tasks and meeting responsibilities. This is best done habitually, through regular check-ins where people state what was expected of them and what they accomplished. This keeps teammates informed of each other's work, and makes behavior patterns visible. It's also an excellent forum for asking and receiving help or additional support. It's a regular reminder that the project depends on a team, not individuals.

Participation standards: Thanks to the internet and related platforms and tools, participation is not constrained to in-person, real-time engagement. But this abundance of options can cause significant complications unless addressed early in the process. A team needs to decide how and when participation should happen. Will it be asynchronous or real time, in-person or remote, all members or defined subsets? In addition to defining the how and when, it's helpful to also clarify participation requirements. There are often good reasons why some team members remain quiet in collaborations. They may be introverts or uncomfortable in group settings. Or more novice than other members and fearful of being wrong. But it does no good to have a diverse team if key members don't share their perspectives. A ground rule could provide space for people to speak up safely in a way that feels natural to them.

Tool choice: Just as there is an abundance of participation options, there is a multitude of tools that a co-creative team can use. How and where will information be archived? Which communication options are preferred? Which development or tracking tools will be used? How will tools be shared and what are the protocols for each? Will training be needed? All these questions need to be answered before a process begins. It's wise to choose tools familiar to team members, but not if the choices are too old or inappropriate for the project. New tools like digital whiteboards, communication channels, and online project management platforms can greatly enhance a team's performance if used correctly and consistently.

Communication guidelines: A common collaboration problem is misunderstandings that lead to mistakes, wrong direction, missed deadlines, and more. The more diverse the team, the more difficult it can be to understand each other, to reach consensus, to build trust among teammates, and to give up control and share power. A ground rule that encourages clear and frequent communication can help remedy this. That agreement can include encouragement of regular habits, like sending meeting reminders complete with an agenda or key questions. Or recapping each meeting with a quick list of accomplishments, decisions, and open questions. Defining common terms like "deadline" or "satisfactory" or even "agreement" may seem like overkill, but differing perceptions are a regular contributor to confusion.

Decision-making: When one person is in charge, decision-making is simple: the leader decides, others follow. In a collaborative environment decision-making needs to be defined. Depending on the team and how

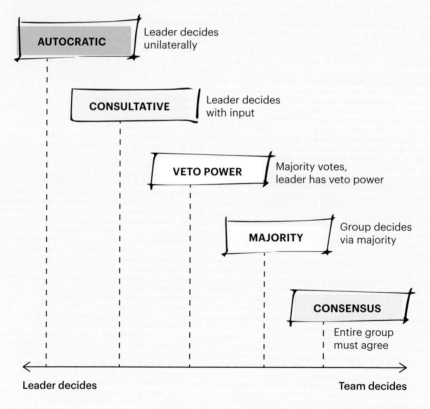

Decision-making spectrum[1]

---

1. Decision-making spectrum adapted from Tannenbaum and Schmidt's leadership continuum model.

it prefers to function, decision-making can be similar to an autocratic style, or it can be delegated. Team members or groups can contribute, consult, have veto power, be consensus driven, or establish a "majority rules" construct. Whichever approach is adopted, it needs to be followed consistently and its output respected.

Conflict management: Ground rules should always include an agreed-upon approach to handling conflict and dissent. There are many good ways to do this, and again it's a team choice, but the process should be explicit. It should recognize what type of behavior merits mediation and how that process will happen. It should also include specifics on what happens after the conflict is resolved, usually an agreement to "move forward" and put it in the past.

Other rules: There will be a host of subtleties and unspoken rules impacting a team's efforts. Political nuances may be more important than they initially look. What seemed easy can become complex when previously unknown influences distort the process. These variables can be addressed through guidelines that are specific to the setting or that develop later in the process.

Choosing the right process and adopting rules that guide and support team engagement aren't glamourous phases of changemaking, but like scaffolding for a high-rise, they make the more exciting phases possible. The reward of taking adequate time and deliberation to build this framework isn't immediate, but it is substantial.

Takeaways

The right process improves performance.
Choosing and implementing the right process can be the difference between drifting, erratic progress and deliberate, steady advancement. The right operating process silently moves action along, giving members a sense of control while allowing exploration of completely novel ideas or implementations.

A design process works well for change initiatives.
For most change projects, the Double Diamond approach will work well with a few modifications. The Double Diamond approach provides the fluidity and iteration that a change initiative demands. It outlines the order of phases and frames their general intent, but makes clear the importance of stakeholder participation and iterative development. It guides experimentation, allowing for inventiveness and learning, and it recognizes the need for a slow, deliberate scaling of solutions.

Clarify the details.
To work as intended, a process needs to be well understood by all team members, and appropriately extended into plans and frameworks. It needs to be steered by shared agreements that confirm progress, select tools and platforms, define expectations for participation and communication, and specify how conflict is resolved.

Take It Further

Agile Practice Guide.
Project Management Institute, 2017.

Creative Selection: Inside Apple's Design Process During the Golden Age of Steve Jobs.
Ken Kocienda. St. Martin's Press, 2018.

Radical Focus: Achieving Your Most Important Goals with Objectives and Key Results.
Christina Wodtke. Cucina Media, 2021.

Rituals for Work: 50 Ways to Create Engagement, Shared Purpose and a Culture That Can Adapt to Change.
Kursat Ozenc, PhD, and Margaret Hagan, PhD. Wiley, 2019.

The Age of Agile: How Smart Companies Are Transforming the Way Work Gets Done.
Stephen Denning, Tom Parks, et al. AMACOM, 2018.

The Design Thinking Playbook: Mindful Digital Transformation of Teams, Products, Services, Businesses, and Ecosystems.
Michael Lewrick. Wiley, 2018.

The Lean Startup: How Today's Entrepreneurs Use Continuous Innovation to Create Radically Successful Businesses.
Eric Ries. Currency, 2011.

The Jobs to Be Done Playbook: Align Your Markets, Organizations, and Strategy Around Customer Needs.
Jim Kalbach. Two Waves Books, 2020.

Chapter 7

Shaping the Narrative

Actions don't speak louder than words. In fact, a change project's actions can be largely silent until communicated. Whether in person or through media, it is communication that informs everyone of key elements of the change initiative. Effectively designed and distributed communication can socialize new concepts and legitimize experiments. It can encourage contributors and participants. It keeps the initiative on everyone's mind, making it easier to integrate into their daily discussions and decisions. Most importantly, communication can unite team members and stakeholders in the changemaking journey, helping everyone stay in sync and paving the way toward a shared vision.

Given its benefits and the numerous options available, developing a communication strategy should be more of a choice than a challenge. Sadly, that's rarely the case. The entire process is often discounted or inappropriately delegated. Change leaders assume that everyone knows what's happening. Or that they don't care about details. Or that communications will be unnoticed or misunderstood or intentionally misused. They believe actions are more notable than words and that their work will be enough proof of competence. This is almost never true.

When there's too little communication about a change project—or when it's not engaging enough—the prospect of failure rises sharply. The team may excel, and the project go well, but without communication, the real story gets distorted. In the absence of timely and believable information, people invariably make stuff up and share it with others. Baseless gossip can run rampant through the most sophisticated of organizations because humans hate information voids. If stakeholders hear nothing about a project moving forward, they assume it's not going anywhere. If they hear only about one part of a task being completed, they believe the rest is lagging. If a contribution goes unacknowledged, they assume it's not appreciated.

Even sufficient communications can cause problems. Honest sharing of questions and risks can promote doubt, causing resistant stakeholders to raise new concerns. Awareness of opportunities can spur others to initiate their own projects, competing for resources. Reports of early successes can overexcite stakeholders, making them expect too much too soon. Communications can be too appealing, generating more inquiries and contributions than the team can handle.

These pitfalls make communication daunting, but they also make the case for doing it well. The benefits of choosing the right approach and employing it in the right way are notable. In-person team communication humanizes processes and builds trust. Visual communications make abstract concepts more concrete and understandable. Networked online communication can rally and unify support. When employed in the right way for the right audience and the right purpose, communication improves the performance and perception of a change initiative.

Ways to Communicate

Everyone knows how to communicate. Most children start kindergarten already able to tell a story, to ask for something they want, and to explain something they know. Few people need to learn how to communicate; rather, they need to learn how to communicate *well*. Sharing too much information bores an audience. Sharing too little leaves gaps that beg for improvised filler. Choosing the wrong words or presenting them in the wrong way confuses or angers listeners. Developing the ability to accurately convey messages and meaning through words, visuals, and other forms of interaction leverages a change team's power and influence.

A first step in refining this skill is to understand the communication options available and how they can be used. To gain visibility, a change team can create an identity that communicates its purpose and intent. To communicate progress and a shared appreciation of accomplishments or challenges, a change team can issue regular updates. To educate or inspire, a change team can present more in-depth information. Each of these options offers a distinct value relevant at different times in the changemaking process and for different reasons.

Create an Identity

Engagement is heightened when issues and goals are made more concrete. Naming or branding a project, or any part of it, does that. While it may seem superficial or perhaps even cheesy, naming an initiative in order to quickly convey its meaning is wildly useful, as former IBM Head of Design Phil Gilbert emphasized:

> We called it the "Hallmark program"—a name that had no other meaning inside IBM—and all of a sudden everyone could communicate about it. I could communicate with our chairman about the Hallmark program or the Javelin program, and she would know what I was talking about. Our senior leadership knew what we were talking about, and the program groups knew what we were talking about. I can't overemphasize the importance of naming things. And creating a communications

program top to bottom around those names. It makes the orga-nization smaller. Changing IBM is so abstract, but the entire company of 370,000 people knew what we were talking about when we referred to those names.

As designers know, branding goes far deeper than coming up with a catchy name. A brand is how people think about a product, service, or experience. Although typically reflected in a name or logo, branding encompasses all assets and values of a product in a way that shapes the perception of it. In the case of a change initiative, it provides the same benefit, encapsulating the pieces and parts of the initiative into an easily understood concept. Done well, it can set expectations, add credibility, and communicate shared values.

Simply by choosing the right name, branding can identify your focus and intent. A change program branded "Everest" implies distinction and dominance. It suggests a difficult challenge that sets the victor apart from others. It can be further extended by using a stark alpine color palette and a confident communication style. In comparison, a change program branded "Kumbaya" suggests community and connection. It implies the positive impact of camaraderie and celebration. It can be extended by a warm, colorful palette and a humorous or friendly style.

When communications adopt brand guidelines, such as using consistent and familiar formats, they improve stakeholders' ability to interpret and accept messages. Using a branded template or following a formula is not lazy. It represents a type of contract between the changemakers and the audience where everyone agrees on how information will be shared. Adopting a branded layout or order of information speeds comprehension and directs focus. Using agreed-upon terminology and other details a brand identity can dictate fosters more precise expressions and facilitates more informed dialogue. If cleverly conceived, brand imagery can ignite emotional contagion and spread memes far and wide. Slap a brand on a T-shirt or cap, and it helps bond a team.

While branding is a creative expression, it's not an unbounded art project. It needs to fit the organization and can't ignore context. Communications must use words and concepts relevant to the organization, community, or movement. For businesses or nonprofits, the appropriate words and tone can likely be found in their documents and digital presence. For change initiatives that are social, cultural, or political in nature, the choice of language and tone is more difficult. While a well-crafted and uniquely appropriate phrase can unite forces on either side of a divide, a poorly constructed phrase can lead to ridicule and early failure. The best advice is to work with a communications expert—preferably one who is a genius. If that's not an option, test the communication on someone who is sensitive to the issues and willing to provide honest feedback.

The overriding goal of creating an identity for a change initiative should be to fit in, not to stand out. Brands that stand out too much send the message that a team is foreign to the organization, often initiating a virus-fighting response. By integrating the organization's content and aesthetic preferences, a brand can reinforce a change initiative's main-stream membership, eliciting broader acceptance.

Update Regularly

Communication updates inform and engage, ideally building support as the change initiative progresses. Whether in person or through media channels, regular updates indicate progress, explain decision-making, and unify support. Design leader Minette Norman considered this so important that she made it one of her top priorities when she was VP of Engineering Practice at Autodesk:

I constantly communicated to my staff. Every month I would do an all-hands meeting. Every quarter, I would do a newsletter internally for my own staff, so they understood why I was making the decisions I was making, why we were investing in these things, and how their work was being represented to the rest of the company. Then I communicated up and out a lot.

As Minette's story exemplifies, updates come in a variety of shapes and sizes. They can be short emails, Slack posts, or more lengthy recaps. They can be brief weekly "check-ins" delivered in status meetings, video talks, or posts on social media. They can be dynamic visuals like heat maps that indicate what is happening in real time. The nature of updates depends on the team's abilities and the audience's preferences, but regardless of how they're designed, updates should always strive to be clear, concise, and accurate.

This doesn't mean that their content should be cursory. It may seem effortless to send quick updates, but they need substance. If you email teammates or stakeholders a list of recent accomplishments, they may skim it. If you explain why those accomplishments matter, they'll pay more attention. Clarifying the "why" adds deeper meaning. Why are some failures expected? Why is this experiment happening now? How will it benefit stakeholders? The explanations may prompt more discussion and even debate, but that's a sign of success, not cause for concern.

Tell a Good Story

Sometimes updates aren't enough. Sometimes changemakers need to paint a more complete picture or share a more detailed story. For example, research findings are usually too extensive to be delivered in an email. Envisioned outcomes need time for debate and acceptance. Results from experiments or iterations benefit from thoughtful interaction on what went well and what didn't. This type of depth is better delivered through presentations, infographics, Q&A sessions, in-person workshops, and more. Developing any of these approaches takes more time and effort than a simple update, but once again, it's worth the effort, especially if the content can be conveyed as a story.

Good storytelling elevates a change initiative from process to performance. It showcases contributors and repositions shortfalls in a way that makes them less troubling. It unites the audience in hopes for a happy ending or in better understanding of dire consequences. Stories simplify complex details, help stakeholders grasp more nuanced interactions, and make them more comfortable taking risks.

Stories are also more memorable. Humans evolved while listening and learning from stories, and narrative continues to have distinct neurological effects on human brains

Liz Ogbu Story

People are human beings that often get pushed into serving in particular roles or positions, and they're not given the luxury to tap into the human side of things. Storytelling tries to get people to think of their human side first, and then their particular role or position in this structure.

The system is set up so that you don't lead with the heart. It's not seen as successful. It's not seen as measurable. It's too wishy-washy, too "feel good," and that does not float in the world of business. So people don't do it. But it does float because everyone wants to do right, everybody wants to do good.

If you speak to the heart through storytelling, it actually is a better way to get people to take risks than if you try to present the numbers game. I mean, I have the receipts so I can back up everything I'm saying in my story, but the thing that gets people to leap is trust, and trust does not come through numbers. Trust comes through the heart. ▲

that prompt positive reactions. When enjoying a story, the brain releases dopamine, which makes listeners remember information more easily and accurately. When sitting with others, listeners develop similar brain activity to each other and to the speaker, becoming more aligned.

Listeners or readers can quickly comprehend and internalize messages delivered in a way that reflects familiar plotlines or fables. A potential misstep in a change initiative can be gently conveyed through the story of the "Emperor Who Has No Clothes." A change that could vanquish a competitor might best be explained through the story of David and Goliath. Because these stories are widely known and easy to recall, people digest them more easily, and they can more easily pass them along to others.

But telling a story is an art that takes practice to do well, and predesigned narratives don't always work. When it's not easy or appropriate to use an existing plot line, a changemaker can get the same value from following three guidelines of good storytelling: fit the need, include characters, and incorporate good writing and polished visuals.

Fit the need

What does the story need to accomplish for the intended audience?

Include characters

Who are the people we are spotlighting and for what reason?

Polish the delivery

What is the level of quality that this story must rise to?

Components of a good story

Fit the need. Stories can be relayed in many versions. Tolstoy's *War and Peace* is a 1,000-page plus tome. The CliffsNotes version shortens it to two dozen paragraphs. To ensure that a story fits the needs of its audience, define its purpose first—what does the story need to accomplish for the intended audience? For example, when you are sharing research findings, an audience is less likely to value details on how the research was conducted than to value what it reveals about the problem. They will be less interested in clever data analyses and more intrigued by the words of other stakeholders. Similarly, when you are presenting the results of an experiment, an audience often wants to know up front whether they'll be viewing a story of success or loss, and what if any benefit it has to them.

Include characters. Nothing increases engagement in a story more robustly than including real people. Humans are inherently interesting as characters, particularly if they serve as heroes or victims. Explaining someone's pain or struggle with a problem makes it more relatable to others. Spotlighting a team member's contributions provides a point of attachment that's more compelling than data or lists. Crediting helpful stakeholders demonstrates a willingness to share the stage. Calling out someone for their brilliant idea or innovative approach can result in a long queue of people or groups newly interested in aiding the project (and possibly getting attention for being brilliant themselves).

Polish the delivery. A poorly told story loses most of its benefits. Vibrant language, attractive visuals, and familiar trajectories that touch people's emotions are a story's secret sauce. Readers may nod at statements like "the context contributes to confusion," but they will openly smile at quotes like "opening my email each morning is like stepping on a trap door that drops me directly into Hell." It helps if a team includes a good writer or graphic designer, but if it doesn't, opt for good grammar, simple graphics, and a rational progression. If a story is presented, its need for polish extends to the speaker. An audience will usually be kind to a nervous or novice speaker, but their tolerance rarely extends to someone who is unprepared. There's no such thing as over-rehearsing. Each rehearsal builds a speaker's confidence and ensures a more natural delivery.

Refine the Details

Choosing the appropriate communication options improves impact, but the planning process includes a few more variables. Whether you are creating a change poster, updating status, or conveying new data, four key variables add to or detract from a communication's influence: the audience, the purpose, the media, and the timing. Getting these elements right can greatly enhance communication's effectiveness, but managing them may feel like speaking multiple languages, as Justin Maguire, Chief Design Officer at Salesforce, explained:

> *Communication style and knowing how to bring people along is almost everything. The channel you use, the tone of voice you use, the frequency you use. Some people like to talk on the phone, some people really want to have face-to-face meetings all the time. Some people live in email. So, the reality is you need to be pretty fluent in all of the variables and have a good ability to figure out who you're dealing with and what channels they prefer. You need to establish clear expectations around communication channels, frequency, and tone, and then act accordingly—even if all of these are things that are way outside of how you like to do it.*

Audience

Identifying the audience dictates a communication's content, media, and pacing so it's an important starting point. Assuming a general audience filled with a variety of people at all levels and of nonspecific interests usually produces milk-toast communication—bland, boring, and of interest to no one. At the very least, change initiatives have two distinct audiences for their communications: the team making the change and all others (including those impacted by the change, as well as those who simply want to stay informed).

As an audience, team members expect more intimate and immediate communication. While the approach can include a wide variety of media, at least some conversations need to be face-to-face, even if that relies on video conferencing. Some communications need to be predictable and consistent, while others can be spontaneous. The specific communication style and protocols depend on the characteristics of the team. The tone can be personal, warm, and encouraging, or business-like and formal. Messaging can be brutally honest or playfully light-hearted. Since these communications directly impact trust and team relationships, they should always be authentic to the author, and never dishonest, condescending, or mean-spirited. Beyond project information, deep dives, and subject debates, teams may also welcome content on more personal issues like stress, burnout, or discouragement, as well as celebrations and fun.

In comparison, communications with nonteam audiences are usually more measured, less casual, and less open. Approaches should be narrower and more precise. Communications should be more predictable than spontaneous. In some settings, political implications need to be factored in. Actions and ideas may need to be positioned in a way that aren't intimidating. You may need to back up your decisions with hard facts and piles of data. Since nonteam stakeholders are not homogenous, dividing them into more specific audiences with shared interests can ease communication choices. Perhaps one group is keenly interested in the project and wants longer, weekly updates, while another more distant group is happy to be briefly updated each quarter. Higher-level executives tend to prefer short, direct communications, while a team of engineers or researchers may want layers of detail.

Purpose

Identifying a communication's purpose can go a long way toward creating the content. Purpose can be diverse, but for a change project, it can often be categorized by its intent: to inform, to persuade, to engage, or to inspire. These intents can be relevant throughout an initiative, but they often align with the beginning, middle, and end phases of a project.

In the beginning, communication's purpose is often more informative and explanatory. It introduces concepts, explains processes, and references supporters. It lays out plans and clarifies goals. In some cases, it needs to make the case for a change, even though it's already been approved by others. As the process progresses, communication can become more persuasive as a team needs to win over detractors, calm the anxious, or disentangle the confused. Persuasive content typically needs arguments and evidence, although personal pleas from a respected leader can work as well.

At some point, the purpose shifts to engaging others. These communications speak directly to stakeholders, letting them know if anything in their daily routine might change, or if anything around them might appear or work differently. Engagement may come through personalization or through interactions like quick surveys and requests for feedback. These communications express a willingness to listen. They say that the change team is not invincible, doesn't know everything, and is happy to learn from others.

In the latter phases, the purpose of communication can be more inspiring or contemplative, possibly even spurring revisions of behavior or beliefs. It can be celebratory or humble, grateful or uplifting. It can reflect on previous actions, pointing to successes and acknowledging failures, or it can look forward, inviting additional rounds, greater scale, or new initiatives.

Media

Media is the means by which communication is delivered. It could be email, social media, a presentation deck, or any other form of distribution that connects the sender to the receiver. Choosing the right media increases the likelihood that the communication will be seen and conveys additional information such as its importance or urgency.

The options are numerous and growing, but they are narrowed by the edict that media should always be appropriate to the audience and the content. If an organization has no standard media it prefers and the choice is up to the team, you should opt for the simplest choice that supports an audience's needs and suits the content. If an audience is spread around the world, asynchronous media will serve them best. If they are not particularly tech-savvy, you'll want to avoid choices that require special technical skills or aptitude. But selecting the simplest media doesn't always mean going with the easiest option. While email and text are ubiquitous and almost mindless to use, they also operate in very crowded fields. Your communication could compete with hundreds of others. Content delivered via novel media such as short video clips, audio messages, or even postcards can break through the clutter.

At selected points, you might want to use evocative or expressive media that has more impact. You can host events to highlight big wins or celebrate a string of accomplishments. You can build exhibits for stronger impact and more interactive experiences. If you're unsure of getting attention, you can create posters and secure them to the back of a bathroom stall door or next to a microwave in the organization's kitchen or coffee bar. Anything that gets the word out without causing offense or breaking the budget is fair game.

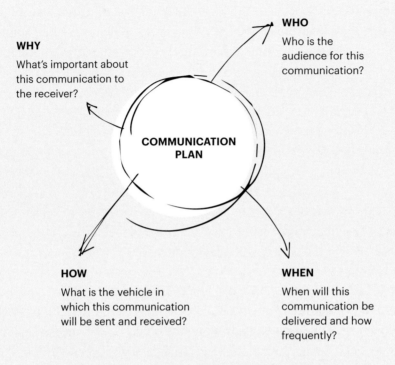

WHY

What's important about this communication to the receiver?

WHO

Who is the audience for this communication?

COMMUNICATION PLAN

HOW

What is the vehicle in which this communication will be sent and received?

WHEN

When will this communication be delivered and how frequently?

Communication plan

Timing

Determining the who, why, and how elements of communication are all important. When done well, they can increase demand for communication. The fourth variable—deciding when to communicate—sets the pacing of communication and meets or moderates that demand.

Most changemakers know that bad news needs to be delivered quickly while good news can be shared anytime. But what about everything else? What needs to be communicated daily, monthly, and quarterly? What needs to be repeated or reemphasized at later points in the process?

These decisions depend on the setting, the team, and the change initiative, but once determined, they should be captured in a communication plan and serve as a guide throughout the changemaking process.

A communication plan reminds everyone of communication's importance and how it aligns with the process. It matches messages and media choice with audiences. It helps keep communications organized and on schedule and makes it easier for team members to share the responsibility.

Plans can be elaborate and multilayered, but a simple one that's sufficiently flexible to track the project's progress is all that's usually required. It's augmented and captured by a communications calendar that schedules messages according to criteria that the team selects, and that specifies the audience, content, and media. The better the plan and the smoother the communication flow, the easier it will be to manage stakeholders' needs and sustain their support throughout the journey of making change.

Takeaways

Good narratives unify stakeholders.

Communication informs everyone of key elements in the change initiative. It can unite team members and stakeholders in the changemaking journey, helping all stay in sync and aligned to a shared a vision.

Create an identity.

Engagement is heightened when issues and goals are made more concrete. Branding encapsulates all the pieces and parts of the initiative into an easily understood concept that shapes perception of it.

Provide regular updates.

Communication updates inform and engage the team, ideally building support as the change initiative progresses. Updates depend on the team's abilities and the audience's preference, but should be clear, concise, accurate, and appropriately substantive.

Tell a good story.

Good storytelling elevates a change initiative from process to performance. It showcases contributors, unites audience members, and repositions shortfalls in a way that makes them less troubling.

Pay attention to details.

Four key variables add to or detract from a communication's influence: the audience, the purpose, the media, and the timing. Getting these elements right can greatly enhance communication's effectiveness.

Take It Further

Crucial Conversations: Tools for Talking When the Stakes Are High.
Joseph Grenny. McGraw Hill, 2021.

Design Is Storytelling.
Ellen Lupton. Cooper Hewitt, Smithsonian Design Museum, 2017.

Radical Candor: Fully Revised & Updated Edition:
Be a Kick-Ass Boss Without Losing Your Humanity.
Kim Scott. St Martin's Press, 2017.

Resonate: Present Visual Stories That Transform Audiences.
Nancy Duarte. John Wiley and Sons, 2010.

The Eloquent Leader: 10 Steps to Communication
That Propels You Forward.
Peter Daniel Andrei. Independently published, 2020.

The Science of Storytelling: Why Stories
Make Us Human and How to Tell Them Better.
Will Storr. Abrams Press, 2020.

Unleash the Power of Storytelling:
Win Hearts, Change Minds, Get Results.
Rob Biesenbach. East Lawn Media, 2018.

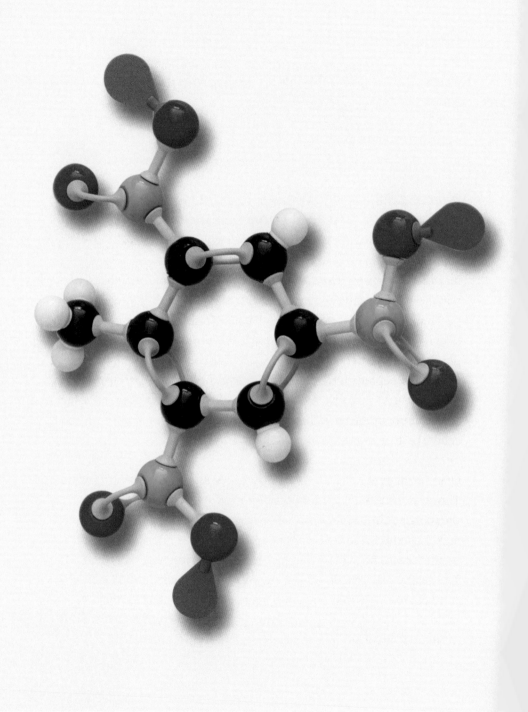

Chapter 8

Building Support

Stakeholders have a "stake" in the change—it matters to them. They may be impacted by it directly or indirectly. They may be supporting its goals from other departments or functions, or they may be on the sidelines only interested in periodic updates. They may be vocally in favor of it or silently opposed. Regardless of their relationship to the initiative, they are integral to its success because change is not just about action; it's also about setting the conditions for actions to work, be accepted, and sustained over time. If you recognize and respect your stakeholders' role, then they are more likely to support the change and spread word of its appeal. Ignore or misread them, and they could sabotage it.

Gaining alignment with stakeholders provides a wealth of benefits. Those who are most impacted by the proposed change are likely to have the most pertinent and informed perspective on its pros and cons, but all stakeholders can contribute. They can help identify obstacles that might not otherwise be evident. They may know of hidden resources or assets. They can make important introductions, open doors, provide cover, and offer counsel. Most importantly, once convinced of its appeal, they can build and spread support, becoming "early adopters" of the change or influential advocates for it.

Alternatively, when dismissed or left in the dark, stakeholders can turn into adversaries. They can exclude changemakers from important meetings or crucial information. They can pull their support or throw roadblocks in the way of any progress. They can mislead on company details, issues, or viewpoints. They can badmouth the changemaker, convincing others that the approach is seriously flawed, or the team poorly led. If powerful enough, they can quietly destroy the change initiative without leaving a trace of their involvement.

Gaining the benefits and avoiding the danger that stakeholders represent requires approaching them with a designer's mindset—seeing them as customers of the change. In that light, they are valuable sources of information, inspiration, and power. Both the change initiative and the changemaker profits from connecting with them, learning what motivates and incents them, and then earning their trust and respect.

Make Connections

Aligning stakeholders and their interests with those of the change initiative transforms them from an indiscernible, immovable mass into a flexible and facilitating web of support. But doing this is no small feat. Almost any size change project has a population of stakeholders, and those stakeholders have varied expectations, influence, and interest. Their roles and responsibilities will differ, as will their reactions. Their political clout may be significant, but difficult to identify. In a siloed environment, they may have conflicting incentives or their own change initiatives that leave them no time for yours.

To connect across this range of differences requires finding something that unites them. Like a star performer entertaining a stadium full of

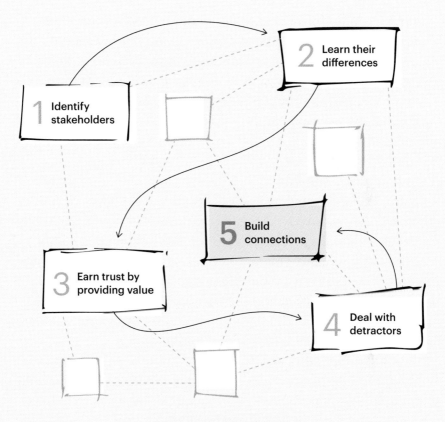

Connecting with stakeholders

wildly varied people, the solution is to find a song that everyone knows and use it to create a shared experience, despite individual differences. To find that unifying song or goal, changemakers need to learn who their stakeholders are and what is important to them. They need to resist the inclination to come in too "hot," trying to fix problems without the proper context or detailed understanding of stakeholders' roles and responsibilities or the culture that surrounds them. Instead, they need to spend time listening and learning, as design leader Dave Hoffer shared:

*I've got to meet all the stakeholders and influencers in an orga-
nization in order to figure out who they are. Simultaneously,
I've got to understand their ideas and examine all of the different things they want to build, so I can figure out where to tread.
Probably lightly at first, right? I've got to take time to understand them, especially in the beginning, because I don't know
what I don't know.*

Empathy and Insights

A designer hired to create a product may have initial ideas of what it
should be, but only a foolish one proceeds without first learning about
the people who will use it. At the start of any project, good designers
seek out a representative cross section of potential customers and use a
variety of techniques to gain empathy and deeper understanding of their
behaviors, their beliefs, and their desires. They seek to learn from them,
to see the world through their eyes, because that view inspires better
concepts and helps them avoid costly mistakes.

Showing a real interest in others and an appreciation for their point of
view is the essence of empathy. When applied to stakeholders, it means
getting to know them as people and gaining a broader perspective on
how they might perceive a proposed change. It means learning what they
value and what they disdain. It means discovering why people might
resist a change that is specifically designed to benefit them. Or learning
that their acceptance is conditional on others' acceptance or on extensive research or on recognition of past failed attempts.

Developing empathy that leads to these types of insights doesn't happen
instantly. It comes from spending time with people, asking relevant questions, listening carefully to their responses, and clarifying anything that
is confusing or unclear. It's aided by an appreciation of human behavior,
specifically how people react to change. Resistance to change is inherent

in everyone. It's a powerful and pervasive force, with biological, psychological, and cultural roots. Because it's often associated with the prospect of failure, loss, or shame, people tend to develop sophisticated and ingrained reactions to it.

An interesting construct of how people vary in their reaction to change is found in the framework of "Leapers, Bridge Builders, and Tradition Holders":[1]

Leapers: Leapers can be fearless advocates of a new idea, direction, or an innovation. They may be natural change agents who believe it's better to take risks and see what happens than to be indecisive and waste time. But their support of change is conditional. They willingly initiate change that goes in a direction they favor, but are less supportive of one they don't favor or can't control. Startup founders are prime examples of the Leaper mentality.

Bridge Builders: Bridge Builders may be open to a change but cautious about how it is designed or implemented. They want to understand its potential implications before offering their support. They are particularly keen to see data supporting the change and its impact, and they want assurances that the process will be well-managed. Because they wait for depth of understanding, they can add value and refinements that Leapers miss. Once convinced, they can become strong advocates and influencers. Researchers, analysts, and professionals who work in regulated or operational fields lean in this direction.

Tradition Holders: Tradition Holders seem risk averse and will be wary of a change, but that doesn't necessarily mean they are out-of-date or uninformed. In fact, these people or groups can be highly competent and

---

1. For more information on this concept, see CRR Global website (crrglobal.com).

LEAPERS

Positive attributes

Enthusiastically helps the organization adapt to new ways of doing things.

Early adopters.

Risk takers.

Negative attributes

Gets bored easily, often focusing on the next big thing.

May become disengaged if change takes too long to implement.

Building support

Encourage Leapers to become the early innovators in a change intiative.

Encourage Leapers to evangelize and share their enthusiasm with others.

BRIDGE BUILDERS

Positive attributes

Deep thinkers who require data to accept and understand the change.

Opinion leaders who make it easier for others to adopt the change.

Negative attributes

Cautious, tentative.

Analysis Paralysis.

Can be slow to adopt the change.

Don't always follow leader's directions.

Building support

Encourage Bridge Builders to research the best way to implement the change and create the proper processes for others to follow.

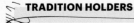 TRADITION HOLDERS

Positive attributes

Champions the traditional values and processes of the organization.

Retains historical knowledge and knows how to get things done.

Negative attributes

Slow to adopt change.

Risk averse, and suspicious of change especially if it's not well thought out.

May become an obstacle or detractor.

Building support

Encourage Tradition Holders to act as watchdogs. Request they monitor processes so that nothing important is lost and cultural values are honored.

Leapers, Bridge Builders, and Tradition Holders

well-regarded in an organization. Typically, they have had a long tenure and have seen similar initiatives fail repeatedly. They may know—better than anyone else—what can go wrong and what the cost of failure is. They need even more data, more convincing, and more transparency on the process. They can be won over, but only if the change respects what they believe and hold dear. Tradition Holders can be found anywhere in an organization, and are common in its highest levels.

Insights like these on stakeholders' beliefs and behaviors can guide new directions or design modifications that will make a change more readily acceptable. They can suggest smoother implementations, ways to avoid or mitigate additional resistance, and opportunities to have more impact. They can redefine the hypothesized problem, revealing unseen connections or complications. Married to an understanding of stakeholders' goals and incentives, they may highlight new opportunities that elevate the change from a revision to an innovation.

Goals and Incentives

Uncovering preset stances toward change builds empathy and refines communications, but changemakers also need to learn about stakeholders' specific responsibilities, goals, and related motivations. They need to better understand how a proposed change might benefit or diminish aspects of a stakeholder's work or life. For example, if employees are incentivized to keep their hours low, they will be reluctant to explore new ideas or try new experiments without a guarantee of success. If volunteers are juggling multiple roles, even a desired change could represent added stress and struggle. If a project manager is incentivized to ship on time, any changes that might cause delays are going to be threatening, no matter how advantageous it might be to the company as a whole.

Doug Powell, VP of Design Practice Management at Expedia, found this to be true especially for those whose goals run counter to change:

We needed to do a lot of work with product managers because many of them were just operating out of fear. They mostly didn't want to screw up. That's a really hard situation in which to make change because they would rather pour cement around their feet than actually take a risk or try to do the right thing, even when they know it's the right thing. They were incentivized to resist change.

Figuring out stakeholders' goals and motivations can be as straightforward as asking them "How are you rewarded?" or "What challenges or obstacles are you facing?" But sometimes the answers are not forthcoming, or they don't really explain important interconnections or distinctions. In those cases, a more strategic analysis helps. Looking at the overall organization and how it operates can add insight, as can paying attention to who gets promoted and why. Pressing the changemaking team to consider the disadvantages of the change or to detail what could go wrong also helps.

Noting distinctions like these leads to a fuller understanding of stakeholders' motivations and resistance. It provides greater insight into how to work with them. Once that foundation is in place, a changemaker can start looking for ways to engage stakeholders in the initiative by finding common ground and shared goals.

Find Common Ground

Getting stakeholders to see a change as beneficial can earn their support and participation. This may mean translating the benefits of the change into ones that the stakeholder appreciates. Or it could mean finding alignment through a higher-level goal that the changemaker and the stakeholder can both support. Design strategist Sarah Brooks explained why this approach matters and how it could be encouraged:

> *How do you piggyback on their existing efforts in such a way that they feel like you're just helping amplify the work that they already wanted to get done? How do you make them feel that even if your idea is somewhat new, it's at least related to what they're already thinking and caring about? Nobody wants anybody else's idea. Nobody wants to be told to do your thing unless it's clear that it helps their thing. It's just human nature."*

To become supporters of the change initiative, stakeholders need to see how it's relevant to them, how it supports their issues, or how it helps build something that matters to them. Without that connection, a resistant stakeholder can be hardened into a full-fledged detractor, working to undermine the initiative and its team. Finding that linkage gives them a path to engaging with the change team and supporting their goal. It allows them to find a role to play in the process, as a participant, a contributor, or an informed observer.

Merge with Supporters

Gaining support and engagement is often an iterative process, one of questions and answers, proposals and counter proposals, arguments and agreements. A reasonable starting point is at the higher, more abstract, level of vision and values. Despite differences in function or focus, a changemaker can look for similarities in desired outcomes or qualities. A stakeholder responsible for community relations may be convinced to partner with a changemaker introducing a new sales process if their agreement is based on ways to improve the external perception of the organization. A changemaker charged with streamlining an onboarding process may win over a reluctant operations manager with a vision of greater efficiency and profitability. These shared perspectives can then be translated into objectives that serve both the stakeholder and the changemaker. While differences will remain, an initial agreement can be forged.

Amar Hanspal
Former CPO and Co-CEO, Autodesk

I think the struggle with making change in large companies gets expressed as people and personalities, but really it's teams that get assigned different agendas. If a team needs to generate $100 million, then they're trying to take every resource available in the company and apply it to that mission. If you're trying to make change, you're competing for the same scarce resources.

This can create detractors who resist change because they care so much about what they're trying to accomplish. Some people are very professional, and they deal with the issues, but other people are much more emotional, and they deal with personalities. They try to undermine your mission, or they try to undermine you.

It's my nature to find common ground and one way to do that is to find an objective above an individual's objective that we might share. I might ask someone, "What are you trying to do?" And they say "XYZ," and I listen closely looking for something in their answer that indicates a common goal we could share. I might say, "Look, we are clashing internally, but if we look at it from our customers' view, they want both of the things we're working on. Maybe we can join forces to try and find that?" ▲

Finding and agreeing to merged visions and pursuits require negotiation and decision-making, another area for changemakers to be sensitive to differences. Some people use a mostly rational approach to decision-making, weighing pros and cons and examining cause and effect. Others use ethical considerations, such as what they believe or what they consider to be right versus wrong, or good versus evil. Still others are more affiliative in their decision-making, looking to see what others are doing and aligning with those they trust or admire. An affiliative decision-maker will not commit to a shared vision until others do. An ethically oriented decision-maker will be tough to win over with a rational argument. An adept changemaker modifies his or her reasoning to fit the stakeholder's way of deciding.

For these agreements and alignment to survive the tumult of the change-making process, they need the support of an ongoing relationship. The easiest to develop is one where the stakeholder and the changemaker "give and take" from each other as needed. The changemaker takes advice, input, and ideas from the stakeholder and, in exchange, offers skills, favors, or similar help. Favors can be simple, like sharing a desired contact or useful information, or they can be more profound contributions, like becoming a trusted confidant or coach. Any skill or asset a changemaker has can be offered, not as a bribe, but as a sincere gesture of help offered in exchange for a stakeholder's time and attention. Dave Hoffer made the case for this approach:

> *You walk into someone's office with the intention of interviewing him and getting what you need. But when you get there, this person is agitated about something. Maybe they're having problems at home or with someone they're going to fire. They don't say what they're agitated about, but they're blocking you—they're not open. You drop your agenda, use empathy to understand their needs, and then you help with that, even if it has nothing to do with why you're there. Because the relationship is more important, building the trust is more important. Whatever it is they need, try to help. You can ask for what you need later.*

Other actions that strengthen and sustain merged goals can be catalogued under the heading of "be appreciative." Being generous in bestowing credit and acknowledging contributions or co-ownership signals gratitude. Keeping stakeholders informed of revised timelines, new experiments, successes, and setbacks reminds them of the partnership and its rewards. Connecting stakeholders with each other and referring to them as part of the team confirm unity. All these actions punch above their weight, helping to bridge the gaps created by individual agendas. In most cases, they work, but in some instances, a stakeholder's resistance is so unwavering that they morph into a detractor.

Deal with Detractors

All change initiatives have detractors. These are people who persistently block or fight a change initiative. Some are openly aggressive in their resistance. Despite a changemaker's best efforts and diligence in finding common ground and securing support, a detractor turns on them in the middle of a presentation. Others are passive—saying *yes* when they really mean *no* or staying silent rather than voicing a concern. In most cases, this intransigence is based in fear. They fear that the change will succeed and cost them power, status, or stability—or they fear that the venture will fail and bring loss or shame to anyone associated with it. Rather than dealing with their fear directly, they lash out at the changemaker.

It may help to be patient and continue searching for a shared way forward, to avoid reacting defensively and continue asking questions and seeking alliance. But if this doesn't work, developing a strategy for how to deal with them is a reasonable next step. A convenient tool for interpreting and addressing resistance is the SCARF model developed by Dr. David Rock,[2] co-founder and CEO of the NeuroLeadership Institute. SCARF is an acronym that stands for five domains that influence people's responses to perceived threats. If a stakeholder reacts negatively to the suggestion of a change, this approach may help identify why.

For example, some stakeholders may resist a change out of fear that it will reduce their status or their relative importance to others. Some may worry that a change will create more uncertainty for them. Still others

2. More information on David Rock and the NeuroLeadership Institute can be found on his website (neuroleadership.com).

STATUS

Am I respected and valued?

What threatens us?

Receiving negative feedback

Getting judged

Feeling left out or passed over

What rewards us?

Receiving positive feedback

Public acknowledgment

Winning competitions

CERTAINTY

Am I accurately informed?

What threatens us?

Unanticipated circumstances

Lack of clarity

Not knowing expectations of others

What rewards us?

Clear objectives and expectations

Making plans

Breaking down projects into smaller steps

AUTONOMY

Am I in control?

What threatens us?

Being micromanaged

Pressure to conform to norms

Feeling out of control

What rewards us?

Having choices

Allowing people to have control over processes

RELATEDNESS

Do I belong?

What threatens us?

Meeting new people who are different than you

Feeling excluded

What rewards us?

Finding commonality

Creating a shared vision

Listening, mentoring, coaching

FAIRNESS

Is everyone treated fairly?

What threatens us?

Feeling discriminated against

Inconsistent rules and expectations

Unequal treatment of others

What rewards us?

Transparent communication

Seeing multiple perspectives

Giving diverse voices a platform to participate

SCARF model

may fear that a change will reduce their control and make them more vulnerable. Resistant stakeholders may be concerned that a change will disrupt their social group and the sense of safety they derive from it. Or they may believe the change is fundamentally unfair and will favor some at the expense of others.

Understanding the range of potential reasons for stakeholders to resist a change and become detractors gives a changemaker more choice in how to respond and more control over how to proceed. Acknowledging these different motivations can help changemakers modify their tactics and defuse potentially explosive encounters. That doesn't mean a changemaker should put up with endless harassment or bad behavior from detractors. While it's important to build social capital and credibility by standing on your own two feet, every changemaker should have clear boundaries on what's acceptable and what's not. When those boundaries are breached, it's time to call on those who have your back and let them deal with the detractor.

Deepen Connections

Learning about stakeholders initiates a valued partnership. Letting stakeholders learn about you builds trust and deepens that connection. No co-creation effort succeeds without at least some level of trust among participants. The closer the working relationship, the greater the need for it. But trust is elusive—it's rarely extended to a changemaker without some test of its merit. It must be earned over time by demonstrating competence and character, as Kevin Bethune did early in his career:

> As a young black male on a high performing team, I had to build trust. I could sense what the crew—technicians and engineers—thought of me. Initially, it was doubt. Some doubted my

intelligence and perhaps my capability. I had to prove them wrong, but I couldn't be the young person pretending to be confident. That would have been the kiss of death. Instead, I showed I was willing to do any and all things to help them. I would roll up my sleeves, clean anything, and learn from Masters, no matter what age. I asked how I could help them be successful? I knew if I did that, their trust would come and eventually, my success would be a byproduct.

Demonstrating competence—the capabilities and expertise a changemaker brings to the initiative—is usually only a matter of "walking the talk." Honestly representing your skills goes a long way toward establishing an initial sense of trust. If a changemaker is new to an organization, competence may be initially questioned by others, but trust will start to build as they gain firsthand positive experience of a person's capabilities and accomplishments.

This is complicated if a changemaker is trying to transfer skills from one domain to another. If you're an accomplished coder, but the change goal requires an understanding of sales, your skills will be less notable. Your management skills may be noteworthy for leading a team of three, but will seem like a weakness compared to someone who's competent leading a thousand people. In those instances, earning others' trust in your credibility, or your reputation for performing as advertised, will take longer. Taking the time to explain why your previous skillset is relevant or how you're compensating for a lack of direct experience can help moderate others' doubts or reservations.

While initial phases of trust are based on functional attributes—essentially, can you perform as required—deeper levels of trust are based on character issues like intentions and integrity. It's normal for people

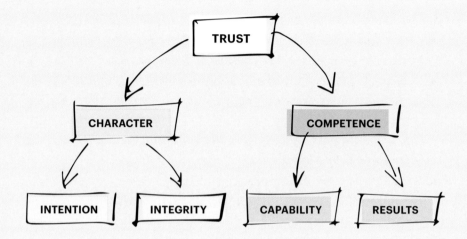

The components of trust

to wonder about a changemaker's motivation. Is he pushing change because he wants to be important or in charge, or does he passionately believe in the benefits that will accrue for everyone? Is she willing to fight the hard battle of convincing others, or is she someone who will take shortcuts that disenfranchise people and hide what's happening? The answers to questions like these are difficult to determine in the abstract. They only become evident over time.

It's also reasonable to withhold judgment on a changemaker's integrity until sufficient evidence supports a conclusion. That evidence arises from a changemaker's behavior in all types of situations, especially those that are challenging. Is he consistently honest and fair? Is she real or playing a role? Those who have spent time in Silicon Valley have run into more than one deceitful changemaker. These are individuals who deftly convince investors and employees that they are brilliantly talented, team-oriented leaders destined to earn their companies fame and fortune. Inevitably, their companies fail, often spectacularly, as people learn these leaders have lied and cheated their way to the spotlight. While these charlatans are thankfully rare, their existence can make people wary of accepting others' integrity at face value. As stakeholders see that a changemaker consistently shows up as the person he or she claims to be, trust builds.

Trust improves all aspects of the change process, but its most notable benefits often arise in times when a changemaker takes risks on behalf of the team or organization. These are situations where there's not enough data or time to evaluate an outcome accurately—or when a decision is needed without strong support on either side. Trust's benefits also become evident when something goes wrong and changemakers must defend and protect their teams, even if that risks negative ramifications on them. These are the times when a changemaker needs to say "trust me" in order to move forward. The bigger the change, the more likely this is to happen. Building an informed, engaged, and supportive network of stakeholders makes it more likely their response will be "we do."

Takeaways

Connect to stakeholders.

Stakeholders have a "stake" in the change—it matters to them. Regardless of their relationship to the initiative, they are key to its success. Include them, and they are more likely to support it. Ignore or misunderstand them, and they could sabotage it.

Understand their needs.

Showing a real interest in stakeholders and an appreciation for their point of view helps build their support. Striving to better understand how a proposed change might benefit or diminish aspects of a stakeholder's work or life can lead to better ideas and smoother implementation.

Find common ground.

Getting stakeholders to see a change as beneficial can earn their support and participation. This may mean translating the benefits of the change into ones that the stakeholder appreciates. Or it could mean finding alignment through a higher-level goal that they both support.

Deepen the relationship.

Learning about stakeholders initiates a valued partnership. Letting stakeholders learn about you builds trust and deepens that connection.

Take It Further

Ask Powerful Questions: Create Conversations That Matter.
Will Wise. CreateSpace Independent Publishing Platform, 2017.

Difficult Conversations: How to Discuss What Matters Most.
Douglas Stone, Bruce Patton, and Sheila Heen. Penguin Books, 1999.

Getting to Yes: Negotiating Agreement Without Giving In.
Roger Fisher and William Ury. Revised edition, Bruce Patton.
Penguin Publishing Group, 2011.

I Never Thought of It That Way. How to Have Fearlessly Curious Conversations in Dangerously Divided Times.
Mónica Guzmán. BenBella Books, 2022.

Mismatch: How Inclusion Shapes Design.
Kat Holmes. The MIT Press, 2018.

Sitting in the Fire: Large Group Transformation Using Conflict and Diversity.
Arnold Mindell. Deep Democracy Exchange, 2014.

Silos, Politics and Turf Wars: A Leadership Fable About Destroying the Barriers That Turn Colleagues Into Competitors.
Patrick Lencioni. Jossey-Bass, 2006.

Us and Them: The Science of Identity.
David Berreby. University of Chicago Press, 2008.

Chapter 9

Discover What's Possible

The temptation to jump into problem-solving is strong. It's a visible indication of progress. It demonstrates ability and validates the ego. But it's a mistake to skip the preliminary stage of fully exploring a problem's causes and examining potential solutions. Without this intelligence, changemakers are operating in a bubble, bounded by their own perspective and limited by their preconceptions.

No matter how experienced the team, their initial view of a problem or opportunity driving change is insufficient. It can't possibly encompass the varied views of stakeholders, and it's likely to miss important clues as to how the circumstances originated and why the issue has gone unsolved or undeveloped. A team's initial view may assume that past remedies will be applicable again—and they may be—but in a fast-changing world filled with novel complexity, that's a risky assumption. Even the simplest questions often have multiple answers dependent on point of view. Research draws those alternative views into focus, giving changemakers a better chance of glimpsing unintended consequences before they happen.

When it's approached in the right way, research provides the equivalent of a topographical guide detailing potential hurdles, pitfalls, direct routes, and detours. It educates the team on how the organization functions and the context in which it operates. It incorporates the world view of stakeholders, who are often the most informed on issues relevant to the change initiative. This expanded frame of reference makes the change team more perceptive and more capable.

Janaki Kumar
Head of Design, Commercial Bank, JPMorgan Chase

For discovery, we do lots of quantitative and qualitative research. There's also the voice of the customer insight work, and we look at different personas as well. We get information from competitive scans so we can benchmark ourselves against some of the biggest players in the market. All of this is informing where we want to go.

The synthesis of all this information—that's where the magic happens. You need the time to really see yourself in the research and try to find out what's happening. Designers have to get very comfortable sharing interim research insights. I have some who are very uncomfortable with this. They don't want the research reported before they can understand it, but when you're having weekly meetings with senior stakeholders, and data's coming in from all kinds of different sources, you have to say "I've spoken to three people. I have 15 more interviews scheduled next week. Here's what we've heard so far." That way everyone gets to know this is not the final report, but it is what we're starting to hear. Then, you know, it's OK to say later, "Interestingly, those three people said this, but none of the other 15 that I spoke to said anything about that." ▲

In addition to informing, research also inspires. It produces insights, and insights are the fast-burning fuel of creativity. Without new intuitions or speculations, most solutions will be an iteration or derivative of past attempts. Fresh perspectives introduce new streams of thought that can lead to more substantive concepts and a different direction.

Despite these notable advantages, research is often skipped, disregarded, or truncated. It's considered a "nice-to-have," not a "must-have"; it's assigned to an intern or given three days on the schedule. Perhaps the team feels they have sufficient expertise for the challenge. Perhaps they fear too much data and information will stifle creativity and cripple innovation. Regardless of the reason, demoting research to a minor role in the pursuit of change is a rookie mistake that most will only make once.

A Span, Not a Sprint

In product development terms, a sprint is a fast-paced inquiry into whether a potential customer likes a particular design. The emphasis is on speed rather than credibility because for early beta products, "close" is good enough. That's not a safe assumption in a change project where the stakes are much higher. Design research pursues a more thorough approach. It starts with a wide search for the most useful, relevant, and valid information, and then continues with a deep dive into the most promising discoveries.

This practice of starting with a broad scan, and then focusing and going deep, is important to developing creative output. A recent study[1] of what leads to bursts of creativity, or "hot streaks," reviewed the careers of thousands of scientists, artists, and film directors. By using artificial intelligence and advanced 3D modeling to identify and compare behavior patterns, they found that sustained creative success is commonly initiated by broad exploration beyond an individual's area of expertise, followed by focused implementation of a selected path. It further confirmed that applying deliberate and narrowed attention to a chosen direction increases the likelihood of discovering a groundbreaking idea.

This is not news to most design researchers; it's the way they typically work. While research is time-consuming, those who skip the exploration or don't focus enough on promising tangents are in danger of producing boring or derivative results, a fate far worse than going too wild. Depending on how sizable the challenge is, the time it requires can be as brief as a couple of months or as long as a year. If that sounds unrealistic, you probably forgot to factor in the time it will take to redo missteps caused by not having the right information.

---

1. "Understanding the Onset of Hot Streaks Across Artistic, Cultural, and Scientific Careers," *Nature Communications*, Sept. 2021.

The Wide View

Gathering and reviewing a broad cross section of information, data, and input ensure sufficient representation and help pinpoint where to go deeper. While all team members should be briefed on research, this initial phase usually falls to a subset of members. Ideally, these are relentlessly curious people who are excited by exploring nuances, confirming validity, and staying open to changing their opinions. If they have analytic skills or interviewing experience, that's a plus, but more important qualities are persistence, honesty, and a sincere joy of learning because this is a time to be curious and gain from others. It's a time to subdue egos, avoid self-importance, and consider alternative options and possibilities.

Resources for this phase can come from anywhere, but they tend to fall into three categories—scans, observations, and interviews. Scans review a wide range of topics and useful contextual input coming from industry overviews, financial analyses, census data, trend forecasts, streaming data, and more. They look backward to see what preceded or provoked the current status and look forward to learn what may influence it in the future. Observations pay attention to how things are done. They look for problems that are evident in behavior, such as how long lines form, where damaging behaviors are supported, or when people ask the same questions repeatedly, ignore instructions, or miss deadlines. Because solutions are often directly related to the workarounds that people devise to deal with them, observing those fixes can provide meaningful insights.

Interviews, or discussions with people who have a vested interest in the change or relevant information on it, are usually the most critical to change research. Interviews focus attention on stakeholders, helping them feel valued and heard. They can identify interesting questions, puzzling inconsistencies, and potential explanations. Through simple queries and careful listening, interviews can add dimension and nuance to a changemaker's knowledge. Through mindful probing, they help discover unspoken or latent desires that people have and clarify their concerns and fears. In some cases, interviews can even introduce new ideas and options that might not have been considered.

The interview process can also initiate a relationship between the changemaker and the stakeholder, one that can grow stronger over time, as Justin Maguire, Chief Design Officer of Salesforce, emphasized:

> *In doing the legwork to reach out and connect and understand, you also build relationships and, at a very minimum, build a measure of trust with those people as you gain an understanding of their world. Too many leaders love the hero story and think it's their job alone to make change. It's much, much better to bring a team of humans together. That doesn't mean you're giving up the right to your own point of view or both, but you're doing it in a way that suggests your way might be wrong. That invites collective wisdom to the table. All of that goes hugely toward creating buy-in wherever you end up.*

Since interviews benefit from diversity and there are many types of stakeholders in any change initiative, it's important to reach out to a range that includes those impacted by the change, those who can contribute, and those who want to stay informed.

Impacted stakeholders: These stakeholders are directly impacted by the change. They are people with "skin in the game"—people who have a vested interest in either supporting or resisting anything proposed. If the change initiative intent is to modify a fundraising process, those who donate and those who seek donations are impacted. If the intent is to improve an organization's innovation practices, anyone charged with creating and implementing new ideas is impacted. People directly impacted by change may be more demanding and passionate, or they may be suspicious or nervous that the transition will be more significant than advertised.

Contributing stakeholders: Beyond stakeholders who are impacted by the change are those not affected by the change but who can contribute to the project. This group should include everyone who might have information, valued assets, or the power to redirect the project. For example, this information might include market data that resides with an analyst or revenue history only known to an accounting executive, cultural insights best known to an HR leader, company protocols practiced by a product manager, or regulatory details only understood by corporate counsel. Because the stakeholders aren't influenced by the change, they may be less aware of how to help, especially if the initiative is not yet visible to them.

Interested stakeholders: A final consideration is the most distant stakeholders, those who are not impacted by the change and not contributors, but nevertheless want to be kept informed. It's rarely evident who is in this group unless they are identified by others. If the company isn't massive, everyone not already categorized could be interviewed. If an organization numbers in the thousands or higher, a more efficient method is to ask the impacted or contributing stakeholders who they think wants to be kept informed. These stakeholders may not be able to contribute relevant insights or data, but they can indicate how the change initiative is being perceived and interpreted by a more general population.

Interviewing these stakeholders takes time and preparation, and there are few shortcuts that don't sacrifice the relationship in some way. There are dozens of approaches that designers employ when becoming familiar with potential customers or clients, but for change initiatives, interviewing stakeholders in person or virtually should provide sufficient breadth and depth. That can start by creating a stakeholder map, a visual tool for identifying stakeholders and their relationship to the

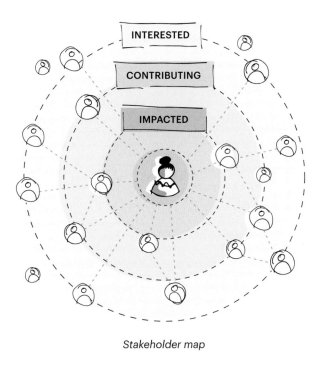

Stakeholder map

change initiative. This asset makes it easier to see who to interview and what topics to cover with them.

Once stakeholders are identified and defined, a changemaker can conduct a "listening tour." A listening tour involves meeting with people who have some connection to the change envisioned, and as its name suggests, placing an emphasis on listening—not lecturing, educating, or influencing. A successful listening tour has at least two goals: to gather ideas, insights, and concerns related to the functional side of any proposed change, and to gain empathy for those impacted by it. A change may promise to increase efficiency, smooth a process, or solve a problem, but those benefits could be overshadowed if the change also makes people anxious or confused. Careful listening can uncover those potential challenges.

When Maria was asked to create an approach to design that would unite all of Autodesk's far-flung designers, she initiated it with a listening tour that took her to offices around the world. In each office, she met with a cross section of designers, asking them questions similar to these:

"Can you tell me your story—how did you get to where you are today?"

"Why do you work in this company?"

"What's working well?"

"What big challenges/obstacles are you facing?"

"What will success look like for you and your team?"

"What would you do if you were in my shoes?"

"How can I help you/support you?"

What she learned from that tour provided her with first-hand information on the problems, promises, and practicalities of each office. That information was invaluable in crafting a solution that would work for and be adopted by everyone.

Interview questions vary depending on the topic and stakeholder, but they should be focused, respectful, and scripted to elicit feelings as well as facts. Probing to learn second- and third-order effects should flow naturally from asking "why?" and "how?" For interviews with detractors or nonsupportive stakeholders, the questions should probe for what is unsaid or explore possible shared goals.

All of these resources provide intelligence that has distinct qualities and serves different purposes. Interviews and surveys are examples of self-reported information that is subjective and may or may not be accurate. Responses are what someone thinks, rather than what they actually do, but they're valuable because they reveal perceptions. In comparison, extracted information is a record of what actually happens. This includes streaming data—hard numbers that represent real actions. Sometimes it's in conflict with reported behavior. For example, an employee might claim to use a centralized tool weekly, but the extracted data proves much less frequent use. In cases like this one, the more interesting analysis is why the employee reported more usage. Was she unaware of her usage? Afraid of ramifications? Intending to use it more in the future?

Because a wide view presents a potent treasure trove of information, it needs boundaries, or the project will stall at the starting point. The goal is not to research every single detail and to have all possibilities thoroughly supported. That's unreasonable and impossible. No amount of research will drive uncertainty to zero or remove all risk. Reasonable criterion for selecting information is to ask if it's applicable, valid, and actionable. While nearly everything can be interesting, the question "How will we act on this information?" is a crucial filter. If it can't be answered, the material should be set aside.

The Deep Dive

Once a breadth of understanding is gained, the research narrows. Certain topic areas become more interesting and relevant, prompting deep dives for more insight and clearer understanding. "Deep dives" mean reviewing thoroughly, but not yet coming to conclusions. It means chasing tangents, re-sorting groupings, or scrutinizing conflicts, and ideally alternating between synthesis and analysis.

"Analysis" breaks concepts or information into their component parts, providing building blocks that can be fitted together to form different scenarios, almost like Legos. Analysis can discriminate between correlations and causations. It can separate facts from any assumptions based on them. It can identify feedback loops and explain how dependent variables influence each other. In some situations, it can provide probabilities, or estimates, of any specific outcome coming to pass.

Analytic results are often expressed mathematically or in charts and tables. They provide proof points and supporting evidence that suggest precision and predictability. Results are powerful because they are associated with the "truth." However, for most people, analytic findings are largely unintelligible and hard on the eyes. Fortunately, the output of analysis becomes less abstract when it's partnered with synthesis.

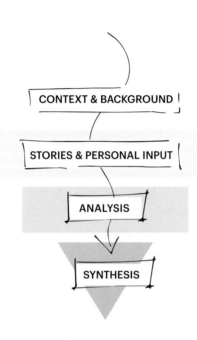

CONTEXT & BACKGROUND

STORIES & PERSONAL INPUT

ANALYSIS

SYNTHESIS

The Deep Dive process

"Synthesis" connects pieces and parts into a whole. It thrives on whiteboards and in workshops, and benefits from full team involvement in speculation and brainstorming. During this process tools like mind maps show up to identify component parts and their connections. It's when Post-It notes become ubiquitous, grouping similar data or identifying distinctions. It's when gaps are discovered and filled, surprises are highlighted, and questions are posed. It takes the building blocks of analysis and weaves them together to see what might work.

Both synthesis and analysis can become formulaic and lock participants into a linear or restricted mindset. This is problematic because inspiration and creativity tend to show up when the environment is more free flowing. Occasionally shifting focus to a more mindless activity like taking a walk, visiting a museum, playing games, listening to music, or just floating in a pool can generate that environment. Anything that is relaxing or engaging enough to stop conscious processing and allow the subconscious to take over for a while is worth trying. This small investment of time can lead to more creative and more engaging hints, as Ivy Ross, Vice President of Design for Hardware at Google, explained:

> *Our unconscious, our spirit, I think knows what we're here to do. And it sends us little hints. So I always pay attention to what gets my attention. I think if you believe in that, the hints come up. And then the idea is, if you're brave enough to follow that trail, it usually leads to the right thing. So I don't want to say, carte blanche as a prescription, "do what I do," but for me, it was understanding the business of life and how we operate—how we operate in this world among the visible and invisible.*

More superficial approaches to research end with the Deep Dive phase. The team delivers their findings and the focus shifts elsewhere. Design research goes a step further, making sense of the information, defining key issues, and suggesting a range of potential solutions.

Making Sense

While the value of research may be evident to the changemaker and the team, it's often obscure to stakeholders and decision-makers. To be useful, it needs to be digestible and comprehensible. It needs to make narrative sense, to fit the organization's view of itself, and to offer alternative ways forward.

As with the wide and deep phases of research, the sensemaking phase also benefits from sufficient time. In this case, it's time to speculate, to ask, "what if?" and "how might we?" It's time to model inputs and potential outcomes. To draw conclusions and then challenge them. To visualize the findings and bring them to life. To craft logical arguments along with clever insights that tie all the research together in a way that others can act on it.

These goals are best met through the collaboration of all team members. Just as diversity aids input, it also improves output. A more detail-minded teammate might note a pattern that others missed. A more adventurous type might risk an association that others find too ambitious. An introvert might see potential where an extrovert sees nothing, and a leader might ignore warning signs that cause others to pause. This activity doesn't need to follow a strict plan, but it does need to turn words into stories and numbers into assets. Done artfully, these deliverables can convert adversaries and win over the reluctant. They can connect opposing sides and defuse clashes. They can increase empathy and sustain support. Ideally, they can move everyone along a path in a coherent and cohesive manner.

Models and Visualizations

Models and visualizations convey information more quickly and clearly than words do, which can push stakeholders to think beyond default positions and conventional assumptions. Converting complex analytics or detailed interviews into a visual form can activate pattern recognition, a powerful ability that connects information received from the environment with content stored in the brain. While this can be done with computers, humans are remarkably good at it, particularly when information is visualized.

Three of the most influential visual tools for change initiatives are personas, journey maps, and storyboards. Personas are simplified representations

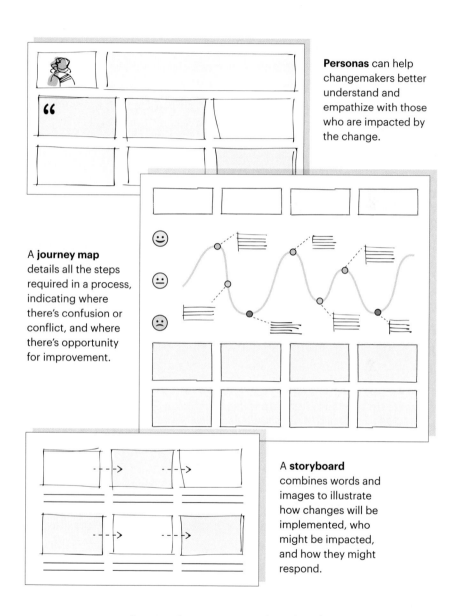

Personas can help changemakers better understand and empathize with those who are impacted by the change.

A **journey map** details all the steps required in a process, indicating where there's confusion or conflict, and where there's opportunity for improvement.

A **storyboard** combines words and images to illustrate how changes will be implemented, who might be impacted, and how they might respond.

Personas, journey maps, and storyboards

of people with similar patterns of behavior and belief. They summarize key traits, goals, motivations, and frustrations that these people share. A well-designed persona becomes the "voice" of this population in discussions where they aren't physically present. In a change initiative, personas can help others better understand and empathize with those who are impacted by the change.

A journey map visually depicts the stages that people go through to accomplish a task or undertake an experience. It represents the patterns of behavior and emotional engagement common to people when completing an activity. In a change initiative, a journey map might detail all the steps required in a current process, indicating where there's confusion or conflict, and where there's opportunity for improvement.

A storyboard uses words and images to illustrate how a change could be implemented, who might be impacted, and how they might respond. It simplifies the change to its most essential parts and can greatly aid understanding. These tools—along with 2x2 matrices, flowcharts, wireframes, and more—transform data and insights into instantly recognized concepts that stakeholders can grasp and follow. They make the findings and the options they support more intelligible.

Identifying Options

One of the most difficult transitions of research is when the speculation needs to stop and conclusions need to be drawn. There's always the fear that something's been missed or that more time will elevate the findings even more. But overthinking is just as damaging as underthinking. Changemakers initiate this phase by shifting focus to the next step in the process when the team uses the research findings as an influence on the creation of a shared vision and its supporting principles, priorities, and projects. Research feeds into that next phase by structuring findings and conclusions into a framework with these five sections:

Summarize the problem or opportunity. Is the originally hypothesized problem or opportunity for change accurate or should it be revised? It's not unusual for research to uncover that the originally hypothesized situation is not fully accurate. An organization might initially think their approach to onboarding is flawed, only to learn that the real culprit is inadequate technology. They might believe their challenge is improving how community members meet and interact, and then find that it's also about keeping that space safe over time.

Explain what created the problem or opportunity. What are its root causes? Why did it happen? This is a critical insight to convey because any solution needs to relate back to an initiating cause. Is inadequate technology caused by scarce funding or insufficient attention to needs? Is safety important because of perceived threats or group values?

Describe those people impacted by the change. Who is most impacted by the problem and its solution? Are there those who are directly impacted and those who are indirectly impacted? For example, in changing a sales process, account executives may be directly impacted, but IT personnel may be indirectly impacted because they support the systems and train personnel. Personas come back into play here, illustrating whose lives or work will be changed, what they need and want, and how they think improvements should be made.

Identify pain points and obstacles. Why is there resistance to change? Where could improvements or transformation have the greatest impact? This information aids in prioritizing what gets addressed and when that should happen. It cautions where more time might be needed. It can also reveal interdependencies, such as when new technology solves one problem by reducing manual labor, but creates another by requiring more trained administrators. Journey maps help make this clearer by turning complex, largely abstract information into a visual flow that highlights where processes slow down or get confusing, where hours are lost, or how people become disconnected.

Offer a range of potential solutions. Occasionally, the findings are so clear-cut that only one solution is possible. More often, there are several possible ways forward, depending on an organization's appetite for risk, available resources, and strategic preference. A simple way to create a range of options is to start with "do nothing" (this is always worth considering, if only as a reminder of why something needs to change) and then offer a series of more significant solutions, ending with an idea that stretches the bounds of what the team imagines possible. The goal with this section is not to dictate what the vision should be or how the team should proceed, but rather to show where there's potential and what is possible.

For this framework and its five sections to be impactful, it should be designed as a narrative. A good research narrative connects human needs and desires with organizational goals. It's easy to follow and explains what is important and why. It conveys the main findings, but also stimulates engagement and encourages sharing. A well-crafted story is repeated, passed around, commented upon because that's what humans do, as design strategist Sarah Brooks reminded us:

> *We think in stories. The deepest level of what motivates us are the myths and worldviews we've internalized as "the way things are." To change our behavior, we need to understand the stories underlying it. And that's work we can do.*

A well-constructed and appropriate research narrative becomes an asset continually referenced in future discussions and decisions. It provides content that can be shortened or lengthened, targeted or generally distributed to fit whatever communication needs the team has.

How to Communicate

How research findings are conveyed can have enormous influence on how stakeholders and other audience members relate and react to them. A standard delivery approach is to produce a deck filled with charts, tables, and small type. That can inform progress for those willing to read it, and it can highlight promising insights or ideas, but it limits feedback—an important component at this point. While emailing these results may be necessary in some environments, archives and road shows offer a more interactive and compelling approach.

Archives: All stakeholders benefit from viewing research findings and extracting meaning from them. One of the easiest ways to do that is through a viewable archive of all relevant artifacts and deliverables. Acquiring piles of disorganized data on a private or unknown server is a waste of time. Its opposite—displaying well-organized information in a viewable environment—helps stakeholders develop an appreciation for its meaning and impact.

A "war room" devoted to the display of key information is ideal, whether it is a physical space or a virtual one, such as a digital whiteboard. Regardless of how the information is organized or displayed, the reigning principles are accessibility and simplicity. This isn't a good time to introduce new technology, nor is it advisable to share complicated analysis or to post opaque graphics. The simplest format and the most common technology keep the spotlight on the information and let it speak for itself.

If it is well-designed, an information archive can serve as a backdrop for all future discussions of the change initiative. It can also provide a quick way for new people to get "up to speed" on the project, and by its very existence, it communicates that the process is transparent, honest, and open to all.

Road shows: Road shows move an archive onto a stage, providing a "real-time" presentation and soliciting others' input. The value comes not only from showing what a team has learned, but also from engaging in a dialogue about that learning. This interaction, although difficult to manage at times, can reveal more advantages or weaknesses in an argument or direction. It may uncover resistance that has been hidden or reluctance that needs to be factored into future steps.

Visuals, anecdotes, and other means of familiarizing data are all helpful. Stakeholder testimonials, whether live or video, can be provocative ways of gaining attention and making impact, as Sam Yen, Head of Innovation, Commercial Banking at JPMorgan Chase, relayed:

> *After I was appointed to be head of design, there was an opportunity to do a developer kickoff. So I'm presenting to 10,000 developers sitting in a hockey stadium. I have 35 minutes or so to talk about the existential need to transform the user experience. So I decided to bring in one of our top three global customers, who was extremely unhappy with our UX. I just gave this guy the floor for 15–20 minutes of that talk and asked him to be honest. As those 10,000 developers listened, he berated all of us, talking about how bad the experience was and showing examples like, "Here's the 20 steps you require me to do." And it was just great. So many employees reached out to me afterwards saying that they were embarrassed for what the customer said and committed to do better.*

Road shows can be fan fests, but they also can bring out detractors. Although it's tempting to ignore people who are unsupportive, it can become an advantage similar to strength-building exercises that are painful to do but add muscle. Being vulnerable to criticism and open to

Maria presenting at Autodesk's Tel Aviv office as part of a multi-city road show.
PHOTO BY VIRGINIE GABRA

opposing ideas often provokes the same in a stakeholder. Instead of continuing to resist or criticize you, they start to listen.

While discovering what's possible is a complex and challenging stage in making change, its goal is important. It initiates the change process. It provides guidance on what needs to be changed and what can be left alone. It prompts and supports the development of a shared vision and its supporting design principles. Its role is not to prescribe what that vision forward should be, or to raise fears and hesitancy, but to build confidence, note cautions, and ignite creativity.

Takeaways

Research informs, clarifies, and inspires.
It details potential hurdles, pitfalls, direct routes, and detours. It educates the team on how the organization functions and the context in which it operates, and it incorporates the world view of stakeholders who are often the most informed on issues relevant to the change initiative.

Start broad and then go deep.
Design research pursues a thorough approach that starts with a wide search for the most useful, relevant, and valid information, and then continues with a deep dive into the most promising discoveries.

Include a range of stakeholder input.
Since there are many types of stakeholders in any change initiative and interviews benefit from diversity, it's important to reach out to a range that includes those impacted by the change, those who can contribute, and those who want to stay informed.

Make it visual.
Use visualization tools to transform data and insights into instantly recognized concepts that stakeholders can grasp and follow.

Share what you learn.
Create a narrative that connects human needs and desires with organizational goals. It should convey key findings, but also stimulate engagement and encourage sharing.

Take It Further

Better Data Visualizations: A Guide for Scholars, Researchers, and Wonks.
Jonathan Schwabish. Columbia University Press, 2021.

Collective Illusions: Conformity, Complicity, and the Science of Why We Make Bad Decisions.
Todd Rose. Hachette Go, 2022.

Hypersanity: Thinking Beyond Thinking.
Neel Burton. Acheron Press, 2019.

Imaginable: How to See the Future Coming and Feel Ready for Anything—Even Things That Seem Impossible Today.
Jane McGonigal. Spiegel & Grau, 2022.

Research Design: Qualitative, Quantitative, and Mixed Methods Approaches.
John W. Creswell and J. David Creswell. Sage Publications, Inc., 2018.

The Extended Mind: The Power of Thinking Outside the Brain.
Annie Murphy Paul. Mariner Books, 2021.

Think Again—The Power of Knowing What You Don't Know.
Adam Grant. Viking, 2021.

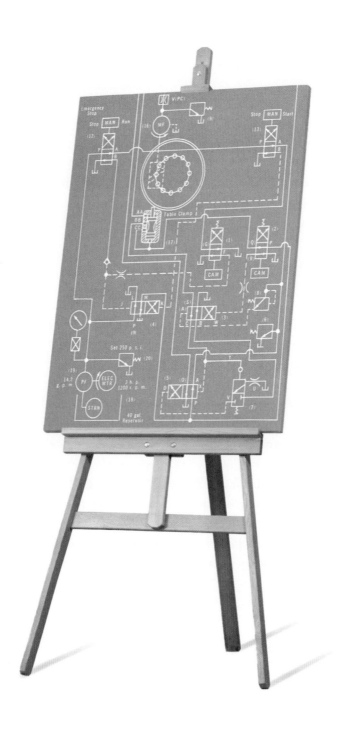

Chapter 10

Envisioning the Outcome

To envision an outcome is to describe what could be and how to make it happen. It's a shared undertaking that involves stakeholders and team members alike. It incorporates the results of the discovery phase, filtering it for usefulness and searching for a viable path forward. It illustrates what is possible but doesn't dictate precise details. It balances opportunities and organizational requirements, and benefits from taking time to discuss, ideate, and define a way forward.

A traditional strategy is highly quantitative and detailed. Instead of a concept or imagined state, it produces a blueprint, five-year plans, and financial forecasts, usually the product of a consulting firm or a select group of analysts. Its pages detail everything that should happen with little to no wiggle room. While thick files may suggest robust study and deep thinking, anyone who has tried to follow standard strategy documents lately confronts their major flaw quickly: they are too exact and unforgiving of any deviation. In a world that is changing rapidly and continually, a fixed plan is a deadweight within months.

Another option—plowing ahead without a defined sense of the desired outcome—leaves the future to chance, an equally flawed approach. With no guidance, a team flounders, never sure of its direction or if they have achieved their goal. Members become confused, unsure of whether their efforts make sense. Stakeholders' anxiety is raised as well, since there is no way to monitor progress and no way to assess success objectively.

Envisioning a change lies between these two extremes—delivering a clear view of the desired outcome but not a specific prescription. It reveals a route away from current behaviors or toward new ones but leaves room for adaptation. It speaks to a broad audience through both high-level and more detailed communications. As a collaborative exercise dependent on cross-functional expertise, it combines the originality of brainstorming and the realism of decision-making. Done well, it paints a future that is simultaneously attractive, viable, motivating, and shared. It becomes something that an entire organization can understand and support.

Kevin Bethune
Founder and CCO of dreams · design + life

I was asked to join this early team working on the vision for the next generation of how product creation happens at Nike. We would create this compelling vision, sell it into the business, and get people to adopt new approaches within the product creation process. We're going to drive lean sensibilities more upstream in the ideation process and drive digital creation in place of what had been a conventional, analog physical creation process. As a result, we're going to see awesome products and all these things.

Well, that all sounded great, but we also had to tell designers that they might have fewer physical samples to play with, and that rubbed people the wrong way. We were going to accelerate timelines, and that rubbed people the wrong way, too. We made a mistake of trying to showcase this vision too soon. We didn't appreciate the investment in transition management that was necessary in order to even get people wired in for this change. We didn't understand that we had to provide enough latitude for the teams we were targeting to have a voice in shaping that vision.

We were just a handful of optimistic, yet slightly naïve folks who had these pipe dreams. When we started shopping the vision around the business, we heard, "Okay, that's cool, but who are you to articulate that? And especially, who are you to say how we should be doing things?" They actually had a valid right to say that. You know, we just didn't realize that change is hard. ▲

Design a Way Forward

In design projects, envisioning is a highly generative process that emerges from empathy, insights, trade-offs, smart risk-taking, and creativity. It draws from research and past experiences but is not limited by that input. Creating a vision takes into consideration the organization's norms and traditions, its appetite for change, and whatever "unknowns" remain salient. The outcome of this process is typically expressed as a concept, wireframe, prototype, or other form that suggests what is possible but doesn't stipulate exact details. A vision is intended as a high-level idea, spurring related smaller projects, initiatives, or further prototypes that can be tested and iterated until they work or are replaced with better ideas.

This same approach works for envisioning change, but rather than producing prototypes or wireframes, it produces a view of the future and guidelines for achieving it. It does this by crafting a vision of the desired change and supporting design principles.

Vision

As noted earlier in this book, a change project begins with a directive that declares what needs to change. A "vision" describes the result of making that change and why it matters. Complaints or concerns that prompted the call for change are recast as solutions depicted in a way that the organization or community can understand and embrace. For example, a change directive that declares a need to modify an organization's approach to fundraising might result in a vision summarized as "We are uniters, working to connect donors with those in need. We believe a streamlined and transparent fundraising process benefits all." The call for an updated sales process might generate an envisioned commitment "To provide our clients with world-class benefits and services and to do so by adhering to the highest standards of professionalism, integrity, and partnership."

While some may disdain visions as thinly disguised internal advertising or a superficial mantra, well-formulated ones can rally support, carefully directing stakeholders' focus and sustaining it through bouts of resistance or times of neglect. It becomes a "North Star," inspiring and motivating everyone to move in concert. By capturing the human value in the change, it creates purpose and meaning for stakeholders. Everyone can see themselves in the vision and how their contribution will matter. By stretching the organization's capabilities and its image, a vision provides an aspirational end goal that helps stakeholders think beyond their current situation, and shapes and directs their steps over the coming years.

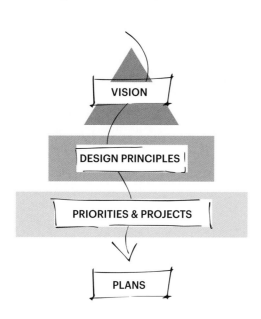

The envisioning process

Design Principles

Design principles serve as guideposts and guardrails for the change process. They explain how the vision will be achieved, clarifying shared values, detailing important constraints, and emphasizing key objectives. Rather than theoretic or universal values, design principles are directly relevant to the situation and precise enough to influence actions. This specificity aids decision-making, particularly in areas where the vision is not explicit.

Design principles set realistic expectations and help ensure consistency by elaborating on the high-level behaviors and incentives that the vision suggests. As the previous example noted, a vision can inspire people by describing how donors will connect more directly with issues they care about after funding is streamlined. The related design principles guiding the development of this vision instruct on what's important and impactful. In this case, they might be summarized as follows:

Put the needs of donors first.

Connect giving with receiving.

Make connecting easy.

Reward all effort with recognition and gratitude.

Build in the flexibility to adapt and grow.

Make what's complex beautifully clear.

Design principles don't detail exactly what the team needs to do or when it needs to do it. That instruction is handled by priorities, projects, and plans. Instead, they make it clear what direction is acceptable and what is not. They serve as vital checkpoints throughout the changemaking process, ensuring that the team's actions are on track and in keeping with the vision. They also signal flexibility. If plans or priorities need to change, or other conflicts arise, the design principles clarify what's most important.

Distributed Creation

Unlike research where success can be judged by the depth and breadth of work and due diligence, envisioning requires debate, imagination, and risk-taking—all of which may seem open-ended and less rigorous. But the envisioning process has muscle. It can unite. It can motivate. It can engage. Because of these strengths, distributing this activity as broadly as possible has considerable merit, particularly if participants represent different functions, perspectives, and experience.

Including a diverse range of minds produces better solutions, but just as importantly, it engenders support. Including others in the process of developing a vision and its components signals that their perspective and input are valued. It also lets them experience the struggle of finding a solution that pleases everyone. It educates them on the subtleties that must be noted and the conflicts that must be resolved. When the output is compiled and shared to get further feedback, their relevance is confirmed, and they become part of the team pushing for acceptance.

As with most generative activity, this phase is best initiated in small, focused groups whose goal is to define a solution or an empowering concept that encompasses the research, stakeholder input, and organizational circumstances. This process benefits from authentic conversations and debates, but it's less a competition and more a collaborative search for the best way to make change. Discussions can uncover flaws and gaps. Examining ideas can find conflicts or roadblocks. Honest dialogues can improve understanding and lead to agreement. Angela Lang, Founder and Executive Director of Black Leaders Organizing for Communities (BLOC), captured this process well in recounting how her team approached it:

> *We got some community members into a room one Saturday. We had our 10 different issue areas, and we had taught our team of ambassadors how to facilitate small group discussions. Each group took a different issue area, and they brainstormed, capturing everything on butcher paper. What do you want to see? What do you want to expand? What do you want to get rid of? What do we want to protect? Then we compiled it all and*

a couple weeks later, we went back to the same group of folks and said, "Hey, now it's on paper. How do folks feel about this? Are we missing anything? Is there something else that should be added or changed?" Then we ratified it as a community group, as a living document.

This may sound like a fun bonding activity, but that impression is deceptive. It is hard work. Even starting it is difficult because it requires engagement beyond the changemaking team. It needs to attract and sustain cross-functional participants. That talent is discerning—they are attracted to problems that are important, difficult to solve, and have few structural barriers. They also may consider how enjoyable the process is, and how unacceptable existing solutions are. If the problem is not as significant as previously thought or not well-understood, attracting sufficient participation becomes difficult.

Beyond engagement, these types of explorations have to be competently managed. Envisioning is not a free-for-all. It is not an ideation session where every notion is acceptable. While ideas are welcomed, their consequences need to be fully explored. Each avenue forward needs to be examined through questions like "What would happen if we did X?" or "How will X react if this revision is made?" The responses may confirm the proposed direction, or they may signal the need for more thinking.

As the process deepens, the group is tasked with asking strategic questions, carefully worded to discover relevant, high-level solutions that can attract diverse stakeholder support. For example, an organization trying to update how its community members meet and interact could ask "How might we best support community members' desire to meet and interact?" rather than asking "Which technology is the best choice for supporting community interaction?" An organization seeking to improve its onboarding process might ask "How might we become a more efficient and effective work environment?" rather than "How can we fix the flaws in our onboarding process?"

This is a time to manage bias once again—in this case, to avoid a singular perspective that leaves out others. It sneaks in because bias is nefarious. It can color discussions or conversations with little awareness. It can be controlled to some extent by acknowledging its possible existence and forcing a broader perspective. For example, a team working on a shared vision for finding a better means of collaborating asynchronously might ask if they're operating from a perspective of the technology being considered or the humans using that technology? A team working on improving an onboarding process might ask if their shared vision disproportionately benefits those being onboarded or those doing the onboarding?

If this phase includes the right people and is managed well, it becomes a time of protected creativity—protection from bureaucracy, from hierarchies, from preconceptions. It becomes a time for stretching and reaching beyond the conventional. Eventually, these collaborations result in a way forward, articulated in a clear vision with relevant supporting principles. But the full envisioning process needs more than creativity and collaboration. Despite the research, listening, analysis, and modeling completed in the previous stage, the way forward is still a calculated guess. To finalize its work, the team needs to make decisions, assume some risks, and outline a plan.

Decide What Matters

At this point, the envisioning process becomes less generative and more decisive. The cross-functional participants are replaced by those who are more informed and specifically skilled at addressing the problem. The change initiative's sponsor or champion weighs in and adds support or redirects efforts. The process shifts to one that is more rational—one that chooses between options and breaks down and examines assumptions, and one that selects what stays in and what's left out. Ideally, the governing philosophy is that of an idea meritocracy where the best concepts win, no matter what their origin, but regardless of the standard used, this team winnows options and makes choices.

Developing a sound way forward often depends on choosing what not to do. While some ideas may generate excitement, there are reasons they aren't worth pursuing. Despite best intentions, it's not unusual for random suggestions from influential stakeholders to seep into discussions, or for research findings to fade and opinions to flourish. Some ideas prove redundant. Others are admirable but unrealistic. Still others aren't viable in a particular setting for reasons beyond the team's control. All these factors need to be reviewed, and establishing criteria for the outcome can help in this determination. The criteria will vary by the initiative, but these general guidelines usually apply to an envisioned outcome:

Directly responds to the change directive or mission.

Addresses issues and impacts revealed by research and stakeholder input.

Offers clear and relevant guidance.

Is mindful of the impact on people.

Is feasible and realistic.

In addition to reviewing options, this stage of envisioning must acknowledge the existence of risks and their potential impact. Research and stakeholder input can't answer every question. If findings indicate multiple paths forward, which is best? If stakeholders have an appetite for new options, will that disappear if leadership changes? Will available technology change and modify the options? The decision-making stage of envisioning must define the elements of the change project that can't be de-risked. It has to list the unknowns and become comfortable saying, "We don't know, but here's what we speculate."

An effective way of doing this is through assumption mapping, an exercise in which the team unpacks any assumptions they may have about the feasibility, viability, or desirability of a proposed vision. For example, if an organization's vision puts donors' needs first, some key assumptions underlying that concept could be that donors' needs can be identified, that donors know best what they need, and that donors will recognize and appreciate this prioritization.

Another option for de-risking decisions is through second-order thinking—considering not only the immediate result of actions but also subsequent effects as well. For example, if an organization's vision is to connect with donors to make fundraising more seamless, the first-order effect may be an improved fundraising system. But second-order effects could include donors expecting more customized engagement, fundraisers feeling less important and motivated, or recipients questioning why they can't connect directly with donors rather than using an intermediary.

These are all obviously thought experiments, but they can be enhanced by probabilistic judgments that identify which outcomes are most likely and then prioritize them by their importance and potential risk. This process, along with accounting for unknowns and risks and applying selection criteria, codifies the vision and its supporting principles. It's then time to expand them into more detailed specifications, including setting priorities, defining projects, and charting a plan.

Projects, Priorities, and Plans

The implementation of change is iterative. It happens in "chunks," or smaller projects that test specific features or ideas. Priorities, projects, and plans identify what those chunks are, in what order they should happen, over what period of time, and with what resources. These are the specifics of implementation, but even though they are more detailed than the vision and principles, they are not rigid. Iteration will likely modify or rearrange them. That's OK.

Projects are small, discrete changes or experiments that in combination will result in larger, overall change. For example, a vision that reimagines an organization's approach to fundraising might generate this project list:

Architect the new fundraising process to outline key revisions.

Reorganize internal teams to align them with the desired outcome.

Review available technology solutions and choose the most appropriate one.

Redesign a public-facing website and backend support system.

Develop a recognition program.

Train fundraisers on the new system.

Educate donors on new ways to help.

The actual list would most likely be longer and more detailed, but similar in nature: a detailed listing of actions the team needs to take over a period of time to transform the current problem into the envisioned solution.

Determining the number and nature of projects depends on the size of the initiative, the team, and the resources. The approach to doing this relies mainly on logic, reasonableness, and timing. Sometimes starting at the end works best. A team considers what the shared vision will look like when completed and then works backward to identify the steps needed to get there. Each accomplishment that leads to making the vision real becomes a project with its own objective and timeline.

For example, if an organization's vision is a more streamlined onboarding process, the team would detail what that outcome looks like. They might describe the outcome as a more automated process, supported by specialists and providing additional benefits to those onboarded. Team members would then scope individual projects to tackle any hurdles or address any gaps that could be in the way of that outcome. They might need a project that closely examines current behaviors and finds better operating approaches, or one that reviews and updates database technology, or one that discovers how these new benefits are valued by employees. In combination, these smaller projects are the building blocks that achieve the vision.

If a vision doesn't require being broken into smaller tasks, but instead needs to be introduced in slower or more controlled doses, then the approach can be one of figuring out how and where to gain "small wins." This strategy was pursued at Autodesk by Minette Norman, Vice President of Engineering Practice at the time. Her vision was to have the company embrace using GitHub, but she didn't push this change as a mandate because she knew most of the engineers would resist it. Instead, she started by working with one of the smaller product groups in the company, engineers who were excited by the opportunity. By prioritizing this project with a small, but accepting team, Minette didn't have to fight off resistance. Instead, she had an enthusiastic group who wanted to succeed as much as she did. That approach kept the effort low and the potential payoff high.

She communicated the initial group's progress throughout the company so that everyone could watch the early experiment. When it worked, she praised the team, rewarding them with increased visibility. She then took on another group and continued the process. Eventually, many divisions in the company bought into the change. Had she tried to get this change accepted company-wide as a singular change—rather than pursuing it through smaller steps—she acknowledged that her chance of success would have been almost zero.

Sometimes the order of project completion is obvious, as in the previous example. Some projects depend on others to be completed first, while others are urgent fixes. But many times, their priority is not clear. Different projects compete for attention and time, and there's no overriding reason that sets the schedule. In those cases, the team needs to decide which projects deserve the earliest or most concentrated attention. The order could be based on size or difficulty, or it could be based on what stakeholders or the organization prefers.

A classic framework for doing this is an Impact Matrix, a tool that helps make sense of competing projects by categorizing them in terms of their importance to the organization and the effort they require. When visualized as a 2x2 matrix, this approach highlights which projects are major undertakings versus fill-ins, and which are quick wins versus thankless tasks. Since the ultimate test of a project is how the intended beneficiary responds, prioritizing some quick wins—projects that are easy to accomplish and likely to please—is a smart tactic.

Since stakeholder reaction is the first real verdict on how the project is going and whether the change will be easy or difficult to achieve, early wins can add credibility and help the overall process gain momentum and acceptance as former Chief Product Officer and Co-CEO at Autodesk, Amar Hanspal, explained:

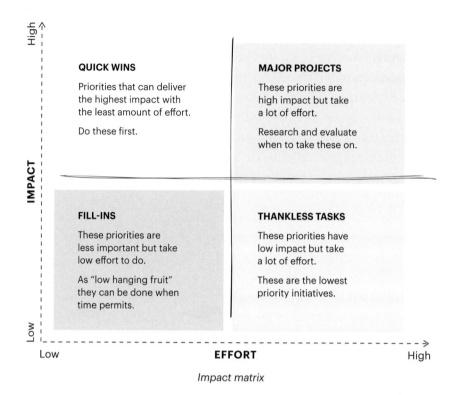

QUICK WINS		**MAJOR PROJECTS**
Priorities that can deliver the highest impact with the least amount of effort.		These priorities are high impact but take a lot of effort.
Do these first.		Research and evaluate when to take these on.
FILL-INS		**THANKLESS TASKS**
These priorities are less important but take low effort to do.		These priorities have low impact but take a lot of effort.
As "low hanging fruit" they can be done when time permits.		These are the lowest priority initiatives.

Impact matrix

You have to get small wins before you go for the big change. If you're trying to drive lasting change, you break it down into three or four steps. Make the changes early on that allow you to leave a backdoor open in order to hit the undo button if something goes wrong. You get an early win with one thing, and you then propagate it to three or four. So that confidence builds and is starting to be about a cultural change.

Plans flow from priorities and projects. Plans take the project list and the articulated priorities, lay them out on a timeline, and determine who will do them and with what resources. Plans also define what success will look like—whether it will have a specific definition or stay flexible, when it can be declared, and what it leads to next. They detail the tasks

of teams and clarify the deliverables. These are the specifics that popu-
late calendars and fill to-do lists. They are the lower-level objectives and
day-to-day actions that gradually, over time and in combination, lead to
the realized vision.

Ironically, taking time to define, prioritize, and plan projects protects
against the consequences of overachieving. Many changemakers make
the mistake of taking on too much, too soon. Projects define boundaries and prioritization sets proper expectations for the team, as well as for
stakeholders. While priorities must align with the organization's needs
and desires, they also need to protect the team, in the way that Catherine
Courage, VP UX, Consumer Products at Google, elaborated:

> *There's always that fundamental problem of not having enough
> people to do all the work that needs to be done. So, you need
> to seriously prioritize and hold your conviction to avoid the
> temptation of trying to do everything at once. It takes maniacal
> focus, and that's hard because you also have to remain flexible
> because priorities will always change. And when they do, you
> have to adapt. But this can't mean you take on more and more
> work. I would rather pick a small set of things and really shine.
> Otherwise, I would have burned out, and I would have accom-
> plished nothing.*

How to Communicate

Communicating a vision and its components is less about informing
and more about socializing. It's about making the case for the change,
communicating the vision, talking to people face-to-face or online, and
addressing questions and concerns. Archives and road shows continue
to be influential and advisable. Visual communication continues to be

important, too, but words become even more critical in their ability to attract and inspire support. For example, explaining a recommended change as "leading to greater synergy" may be easier to accept than saying it will "eliminate redundancies" or "reduce overhead." This is not giving anyone permission to lie or conceal; rather, it is underlining the importance of choosing words and phrases carefully, so they accurately convey the vision in its fullest intent.

Doug Powell, Vice President, Design Practice Management at Expedia, made this same argument, in his case singling out one word as embodying the essence of a vision:

> *When I look back at the change journey at IBM—what's been done and the moves that have been made—they all tie back to the mission to create a sustainable culture of design and design thinking at IBM. That word "sustainable" is a really important one because it means that we were not just trying to change for the moment or to create some condition that can be measured in a six- or twelve-month or even three-year time span. We were making long moves and playing a long game.*

A vision may be detailed on several pages, but it's wise to capture it in a concise high-level phrase such as "Black Lives Matter" or "Ideas Worth Spreading." These short statements motivate and excite, but also communicate the heart of the change. Capturing a vision in a simple but memorable phrase can trigger recall of the initiative in the mind of everyone that reads it.

Since design principles guide behavior in instances where rules are vague and choices are challenging, they typically need to be more fully articulated than the vision they support. But they, too, should have a truncated, more visual version that conveys their intent quickly.

Several design tools can aid in communicating a newly developed vision. As noted earlier, storyboarding, a technique that combines words and images to illustrate progressive actions, can illustrate how changes will be implemented, who might be impacted, and how they might respond. It can help explain challenges and consequences not readily evident through conversation or too extensive to articulate simply. Similarly, posters, infographics, or other types of impactful imagery can paint a picture of what the change means to the organization. Personas and journey maps can also be repurposed from research. More detailed visuals like an outcome map, Kanban framework, roadmaps, or flowcharts may be appropriate for select audiences.

The output of these tools and techniques can improve communication of the vision to stakeholders who gather in "all-hands" meetings, or similar events, that help them learn and internalize new ideas and outcomes. The goal of these events is to foster familiarity and support for the vision and its design principles, and to explain the priorities, projects, and plans. Ideally, these communications entice acceptance by demonstrating why the vision is appropriate, how it will lead to an improved outcome, and when and where it will happen. If the process has been collaborative and cross-functional, stakeholders will recognize their input and appreciate the shared nature of this phase.

Communicating a vision and its supporting components does not declare victory or indicate a conclusion; instead, as Minette's earlier story indicates, it initiates a stream of experiments, pilots, and prototypes—some that will be clear wins, others that will be clear failures, and most that will land somewhere in-between these extremes. The envisioning process sets these next activities in motion and defines their direction.

Takeaways

Look ahead.

Envisioning an outcome describes what could be and develops a strategy for making it happen. It's a shared undertaking that involves stakeholders and team members alike.

Create guidance.

Design principles set realistic expectations and help ensure consistency by elaborating on the high-level behaviors and incentives that the vision suggests.

Make the hard decisions.

Developing a sound way forward often depends on choosing what not to do. While some ideas may generate excitement, there are reasons they aren't worth pursuing.

Sweat the details.

Priorities, projects, and plans identify what needs to be done, in what order, over what period of time, and with what resources.

Take It Further

Designing for Growth: A Design Thinking Tool Kit for Managers.
Jeanne Liedtka and Tim Ogilvie. Columbia
Business School Publishing, 2011.

Good Strategy/Bad Strategy: The Difference and Why It Matters.
Richard Rumelt, Sean Runnette, et al. Currency, 2011.

Principles: Life and Work.
Ray Dalio. Simon & Schuster, 2017.

Project Management All-in-One For Dummies.
Stanley E. Portny. For Dummies, 2020.

***Start with the Vision: Six Steps to Effectively Plan,
Create Solutions, and Take Action.***
Steven Shallenberger and Rob Shallenberger. Star Leadership LLC, 2020.

***The Creativity Leap: Unleash Curiosity, Improvisation,
and Intuition at Work.***
Natalie Nixon. Berrett-Koehler Publishers, 2020.

Your Next Five Moves: Master the Art of Business Strategy.
Patrick Bet-David. Gallery Books, 2020.

Chapter 11

Learning What Works

Complex problems can't be solved through a linear process. They can't be dissected and their solutions pieced together. They're emergent and evolve in unpredictable ways. Ironically, Steve Jobs, the man most regard as a singular genius who could magically turn visions into products, knew that the process was more involved:

> *There's just a tremendous amount of craftsmanship in between a great idea and a great product. And as you evolve that great idea, it changes and grows. It never comes out like it starts because you learn a lot more as you get into the subtleties of it. And you also find there are tremendous trade-offs that you have to make.*

Exactly right. To solve complex problems and make lasting change in a disrupted and diverse setting requires trial-and-error intertwined with stakeholder feedback. As teams experiment and learn, unforeseen hurdles can arise, and trade-offs become necessary. As a result, the vision might be refined, the design principles shifted, and the initiative revisited. Approached with the right mindset and process, these aren't signs of failure, but rather indications of where and how improvement can happen.

Some may prefer a more concrete goal or a set outcome, but that's unrealistic when a change initiative must balance conflicting needs, accept feedback, and remain conscientious of other constraints. An iterative development process, properly scoped and pursued, promotes progress over perfection and makes lasting change more likely.

Iterative Development

Iterative development is a cyclic process of experimenting in small, easily managed attempts, analyzing the results, and making refinements based on relevant input. Each iteration informs the team and evolves the design, improving its quality, function, and appeal, until an ideal solution is reached. This approach, common to design and software development, is a practical way of testing what works without incurring high costs. It can be done at any time but is most efficient in early stages. It can focus on single variables, features, or components. Like AB testing, multiple options can compete against each other, and a "winner" can be identified.

The size and nature of these experiments depend on the initiative, the team, and its resources. If a changemaker is working alone or resources are constrained, the experiments will need to be smaller. If time is limited or the challenge is more complex, they may need to be larger. Ideally, these iterations are public. They aren't skunk works or secret teams, but rather visible attempts at making change that others can see and follow. That doesn't mean they are center stage or in need of constant attention, but operating in secret undercuts trust and raises suspicion.

Regardless of size, complexity, or visibility, the process follows the same pattern: testing or piloting a change, getting feedback, making suggested corrections, and retesting until the results are welcome enough to expand the experiment to more groups or more consequential settings.

Pilots and Pivots

To "pilot" means to test something in a rudimentary form or limited instance to see if it works as envisioned before investing in more development. This is a standard practice among startups and other entrepreneurial ventures where organizations want to take risks, but not ones that will doom them. They pilot to proceed with caution and avoid significant missteps, to articulate the vision, and to confirm assumptions.

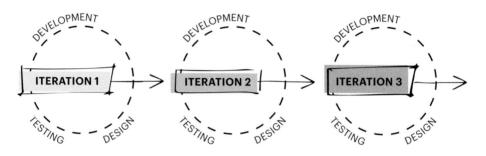

Iterative development

Piloting starts by breaking envisioned projects into discrete experiments. These smaller tests become individual projects with their own goals. For example, an organization attempting to streamline their onboarding process could create multiple pilots testing different aspects of that change. They could pilot a communication revision, a tracking revision, a small reorganization, or a new approach to planning. Each pilot adds information and shapes the eventual outcome.

Pilots aid decision-making, particularly in environments where stakeholders don't agree on how to proceed, or where there's not enough information to implement a specific solution confidently. They can clarify unseen problems early enough for them to be fixed or avoided. It's also a way of building support and engagement among stakeholders. Because they are temporary by nature, pilots are a less threatening way to implement change. They don't carry the menace of permanent disruption. There's an implicit promise that if the experiment doesn't work, the solution will be revised. The pilots can be tweaked or stopped if not working as intended. Because of this, they can be the easiest way to resolve disagreements, as Stanford lecturer Christina Wodtke explained:

> *I was working with this product manager, and I was convinced one design was perfect. The PM was arguing for copying Google at the time, right? He was almost in tears, he was so exhausted from fighting with me. He said "Could we please just try my idea?" I thought, how unfair am I to not even explore it? I'm so busy convincing him, I'm not listening to him at all. So, I agreed. After we did that, he looked at his and he looked at mine and said, "Is there something in between?" I realized my willingness to listen to him gave him permission or space to listen to me.*

The long list of benefits that iterative development conveys masks its primary weakness: it's a process most assume they can do easily. Few grasp its difficulty until they are neck-deep in unsorted details, incomplete tasks, and negative feedback. In any change initiative, there are dozens of variables to try, assess, and revise. They may act one way individually and a different way in combination with other variables. Experiments may lead down a path that dead-ends, requiring a return to start. A successful experiment with one variable may be compromised by a failed experiment with another. Feedback may be bifurcated or conflicting. In other words, there are a lot of moving pieces, and they all merit attention. Keeping track of what was tested, how it performed, what reactions it elicited, what revisions were made, and similar considerations is a full-time job for the most organized person on the team.

Another demanding aspect of pilot projects is the need to set conditions as close to real as possible. The more realistic a pilot is, the more valid its conclusion will be. As an example, the many Web3 community pilots occurring now that involve money or real incentives will be more accurate than similar projects modeled by computer because they include the variable of human nature (which remains difficult to emulate). Making their experiments real leads to more nuanced, insightful, and applicable results.

Make It Real

Often, what people say they want and what they really want are different. Not because they are uninformed or intentionally misleading, but rather because it's difficult to imagine how a solution to a complex problem will work in real life. What seems ideal in theory proves less so when enacted. Sometimes, a solution causes other problems. Or it serves people in disproportionate ways, favoring some over others. Or it works under some conditions but not others. The variables are too great for most people to evaluate adequately until they have something real to which they can react. But real is expensive and often impossible in the early stages of testing and experimenting. Prototypes are the next best thing.

Prototyping is the process of making a rough representation of something, usually to explain its features or to test viability or appeal. Prototypes are particularly useful in uncovering needs or fears that are not evident. By making an abstract idea real, prototypes stimulate more realistic responses. They can also build trust and lower resistance as design leader Dave Hoffer's team did:

> *My team stayed up nights and weekends to put together this crazy prototype—70 screens in a mobile app—a really robust prototype. Until people had it in their hands, everything was a bit abstract. Details had been discussed verbally and recorded on the whiteboard. The idea had been delivered as charts and graphs and in typical PowerPoint decks, all with good data behind it, and all with the best intentions. But once we put that prototype in their hand, their eyes lit up. They said "Wow,*

you made it real," and "Oh, this is amazing. This is wonder-ful." There was huge praise, and the middle management folks backed off, saying, "Now we understand the power of what you were talking about and how you applied it to the project."

The process of prototyping an idea or object usually starts with the lowest resolution approach possible, perhaps a sketch or a loosely described concept. With each test, the prototype can be refined, growing in detail and functionality. That's challenging, but a wealth of prototyping tools makes this process more feasible. In the case of change initiatives, how to prototype depends on what is being tested. For example, if the goal is to change a company's innovation process, it might be easier to prototype it by having a new approach tested by one team and then compared to other teams who continue innovating in the traditional way. Alternatively, several teams might try the new approach, but only for two months as an experiment. Everyone's experience with the new approach can be compared to the one they had previously used.

A prototype can also be developed as an MVP, or *minimum viable product*. An MVP is a prototype that is fully functional but includes only those features that are essential to proving its viability and appeal. This is particularly useful if an envisioned change depends on a new application or tool. If a team is testing how to modernize their sales process, a manually updated dashboard prototype might be all that's needed to gather initial feedback. Going to the cost and effort of creating a fully operational dashboard before understanding how it can best be used could be a recipe for rejection.

For designers, prototyping is a way of thinking. As they prototype, their ideas and concepts become more concrete. The act of making a prototype can help them sharpen or reimagine their ideas. They expect complaints or concerns, but they use that feedback to improve the next version.

Determine What Works

Since the main point of pilots and prototypes is to test reactions, a crucial part of this process is regular communication and feedback from those who may be impacted. Unqualified successes are rare in the initial stages of testing. The bulk of the feedback may focus on points of failure, how it needs to be revised, and what unanticipated problems it generated. As painful as this can be, that's not a bad outcome if it leads to refinements and improvements.

Designers experience this type of feedback early through a process known as a "crit" (short for "critique"). In a crit, a designer presents his or her work to a group of more experienced professionals who then point out what they like about the work and where it falls short of its objectives. A good crit results in a group conversation with the goal of improving a design, not simply judging it as good or bad. Despite rules established to protect the designer's confidence and self-esteem, crits can be brutal. If you've worked for weeks or months on a project, hearing comments like "I'm not sure what you're trying to convey," or "This doesn't really stand out from what's already been done" can be deflating. But learning to accept feedback and to consider differing perspectives without feeling defeated strengthens a designer's skill and builds resilience. Each future crit becomes easier to navigate, more interactive, and potentially more useful. It also teaches the recipient that much of the value in feedback is what it reveals about the giver. It shows their perspective, which may or may not be accurate, but is almost always important.

Get Feedback

Engaged feedback from those impacted by the experiments or prototypes is essential in this phase and it can be solicited in many ways. Brief interviews with selected stakeholders work well if structured and conducted appropriately. Surveys can work if they're very short and targeted.

Defining participants as an "expert panel" on the implementation and engaging with them in brief weekly feedback sessions can also be attractive. While keeping the approach easy matters, even more important is that those who participate give feedback that is honest and relevant, and that team members treat that feedback seriously.

Stakeholders should be encouraged to give candid and individual responses, explaining what worked and what didn't. They should be prompted to suggest revisions, even though most may not be able to do this. Ground rules should be established to provide psychological safety for all involved—for example, directing feedback at the idea, not the changemaker or starting with positive comments, not negative ones.

An entertaining approach to feedback is to gamify it. That tactic not only makes it more enjoyable for everyone, but it can also elicit better information if everyone understands and accepts the context. For example, the red team/blue team exercise employed to test security systems can be repurposed to expose the pros and cons of a prototype. One team of stakeholders (red) can be asked to attack a prototype, while another team (blue) defends it against the attacks. Another game that can increase honest feedback when there are multiple prototypes is "pretend VC." Stakeholders are asked to invest a million fake dollars in the prototype they find most viable and interesting, detailing the reasons this version attracted them.

Regardless of how feedback is gained, it should be tracked, organized, shared with all team members, and archived for reference. Comments can be noted and categorized on a shared document, with resulting decisions or actions noted alongside them. This practice not only communicates an interest in getting feedback, but it also demonstrates a commitment to acting on those comments. That simple designation is both true and encouraging. Most importantly, feedback should be

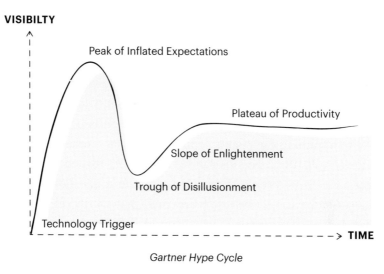

VISIBILTY

Peak of Inflated Expectations

Plateau of Productivity

Slope of Enlightenment

Trough of Disillusionment

Technology Trigger

TIME

Gartner Hype Cycle

regarded as an asset—reviewed, respected, and fully considered in the next round of revision.

Course Correct

The main point of iterative design is to eventually get to a successful implementation through a series of successes and failures. While effective, this process of small gains and regular pushback can be depressing. In many ways, its trajectory resembles the Gartner Hype Cycle, a pattern of reactions common to new technology where ideas initially inflate expectations, then create disillusionment when they fail, but eventually find acceptance over time.

Similarly, change ideas may seem remarkable when they're first envisioned, thus inflating expectations. Piloting or prototyping them introduces realistic concerns and constraints, often dragging enthusiasm down. But persistence pays off. If iterations continue, eventually a version gains acceptance. Identifying this acceptable version depends on examining what's working and what's not, listening to feedback, and course correcting with each iteration.

Course correcting does not mean simply trying any new approach. Each new approach the team tries is dependent on the outcome and the feedback from the previous attempt. To ensure that continuity, the team needs to carefully track what was tried, where it succeeded or failed, and what those impacted by it felt and thought about it. Like an Agile retrospective practice, the appropriate course correction is best determined by closely examining the results of the pilot: What worked well? What didn't work well? What actions can we take going forward to improve the next pilot or prototype? If the answer to these questions confirms that the pilot's key objectives are being met, that merits celebration. If key objectives aren't yet being met, the most likely reason may surface through these additional queries:

Are stakeholders' reactions surprising or different from what was expected? Are there missing variables or insights? If so, more research may be needed or a deeper appreciation of stakeholder input.

Is acceptance slower than expected? What specifically is slowing it down? The team may need to make appropriate adjustments to the timeline and be a bit more patient.

Is there new competition, new leadership, new technology, or some other variable not accounted for in the original strategy? Are the goals and objectives set still realistic or has the environment changed? If so, you might need to revisit the vision, principles, or priorities.

Is someone or some group resisting the change? Despite efforts to align everyone, it's common for people to hide their distrust or lack of support for a change. If they can't stop the change during the planning phase, they may wait until it's being tested and work to make it fail at that time.

How to Communicate

At this point, communication adopts two additional goals: showcasing pilots in process or recently completed, and enticing stakeholders to participate in upcoming tests. Communicating other aspects of the initiative is still important, but this stage offers the prospect of constant improvement and building enthusiasm and momentum by highlighting achievements, insights, and opportunities. Showcasing the actions and outcomes of stakeholders willing to participate in early experiments may win over the curious and possibly even entice the skeptics. Whether these communications are texted, emailed, or presented is less a concern than that they be timely. Hearing about a trial a month after it happened is less engaging than hearing it more immediately. If your communication strategy is set at one communication a month, these announcements can be the exception.

Showcase pilots: To "showcase" means to let stakeholders know what's being tested, how it's being piloted or prototyped, and when results will be available. Showcasing results means celebrating "wins" or deconstructing failures. Each of these are important messages to convey as broadly, as reasonably, and as concisely as possible. It's tempting to make pilot project communications lengthy and detailed because those details seem important to the team. But realistically, stakeholders will glance at the multiple paragraphs and click "archive" or "delete" because those details are rarely important to them. What they want to know can be summarized in the question, "Why should I care?" This can be addressed by briefly explaining key points. A final line can encourage anyone with questions to ask them.

An easy way to communicate without many words is through photos. If the pilot project lends itself to visual capture, one or two photos can quickly convey what's being tested, that participants are willing and excited, where the experiment is happening, and how it's being implemented. Another visual option is to use graphics that convey metrics or other measures of completion, involvement, or success. Personal stories—like the ones included in this book—are also effective, particularly if they are amiable, funny, or insightful.

Communicating and showcasing successful results are joys compared to most missives, but they can go wrong as well. Success is doubted if it's too one-sided, and if seemingly nothing went wrong. Adding a line or two that shares missteps, course-corrections, or early failures that ensured later success increases believability. This is also the prime opportunity for making stars out of those who participated in the pilot, making it clear that the changemaker is not trying to claim full credit.

Entice participation: Nothing is quite as compelling to people as the prospect of being a hero or star. Communicating about a pilot project's success, and heralding the work of individual contributors, can attract new participants for the next round of experiments. While you're not promising a future success, you are offering the possibility of it, and that's often enough to overcome stakeholders' doubts or resistance.

Championing and rewarding the process, rather than the outcome, communicate the iterative nature of implementation. This process reminds everyone that patience and persistence are essential parts of making change, and individual contributions matter, as Autodesk's former Chief Product Officer and Co-CEO, Amar Hanspal, shared:

> *The one thing that really matters that I didn't do enough was to celebrate wins. The act of standing somebody up and saying, "Hey, this was a big win," is one of the best communication things you can do. If you don't do this, then people think that all you reward people for is getting things done.*

If public celebration is not possible or desirable, consider other forms of enticement. Customers are enticed to participate in design research with the offer of a prize drawing or a cash reward. Interns are enticed with the offer of experience or customized training. Awards, flowers, certificates, food, virtually any legal and ethical offering is fair game.

Celebrating a job well done at Autodesk.
PHOTO BY RICHARD HOWARD

For example, during a time of excessive workload at Christopher's firm, the people charged with keeping colleagues happy and collaborative worried that the pace of work was eroding relationships and casual sharing of ideas and learnings. They decided to pilot a weekly "Happy Hour" event where all employees could pause work on Friday afternoon and gather in a conference room for free beer and refreshments. The trial failed to attract more than a handful of people, but the person leading this endeavor refused to give up. The next week she piled all the beer and food on a cart and wheeled it through the offices. She would park the cart in front of each person's desk, prompting them to stop working for a brief time. In this case, the enticement not only worked, but also became the change—the "rolling beer cart" became a weekly event that helped everyone pause, laugh, and reconnect.

It would be nice if all projects ended this well, but that's a fantasy. When projects don't end in success, showcasing and enticements become more complex and difficult to pull off. The effort is still important—it just requires more thought and creativity.

Takeaways

Learn to iterate.
Solving complex problems and making lasting change in a disrupted and diverse setting requires trial-and-error intertwined with stakeholder feedback.

Repeat until successful.
Iterative development is a cyclic process of experimenting in smaller, easily managed attempts at change, analyzing the results, and making refinements based on relevant input. Each iteration informs the team and evolves the design, improving its quality, function, and appeal, until an ideal solution is reached.

Build support.
Pilots and prototypes aid decision-making and clarify unseen problems early enough for them to be fixed or avoided. It's also a way of building support and engagement among stakeholders. Since the main point of pilots and prototypes is to test reactions, a crucial part of this process is regular communication and feedback from those who may be impacted.

Celebrate wins.
Championing and rewarding the process, rather than the outcome, communicates the iterative nature of implementation. It reminds everyone that patience and persistence are an essential part of making change and individual contributions matter.

Take It Further

Beyond the Prototype: A Roadmap for Navigating the
Fuzzy Area Between Ideas and Outcomes.
Douglas Ferguson. Voltage Control, 2019.

How to Listen with Intention: The Foundation of True
Connection, Communication, and Relationships.
Patrick King. Independently published, 2020.

Little Bets: How Breakthrough Ideas Emerge
from Small Discoveries.
Peter Sims. Free Press, 2011.

Noise: A Flaw in Human Judgment.
Daniel Kahneman, Olivier Sibony, and Cass
R. Sunstein. Little, Brown Spark, 2021.

Sprint: How to Solve Big Problems and
Test New Ideas in Just Five Days.
Jake Knapp, John Zeratsky, and Braden Kowitz. Simon & Schuster, 2016.

The Scout Mindset: Why Some People See Things Clearly
and Others Don't.
Julia Galef. Portfolio, 2021.

Trial, Error, and Success: 10 Insights into Realistic Knowledge,
Thinking, and Emotional Intelligence.
Sima Dimitrijev and Maryann Karinch. Armin Lear Press, 2021.

Chapter 12

When Things
Go Wrong

Failure stalks a change initiative. Even with all the right qualifications, a leader can stumble. The team can become dysfunctional. The company can resist. The circumstances can change. In each case, failure can be the fault of people, processes, perceptions, or pacing. These dangers can be significantly moderated by an adept changemaker, but never completely prevented. Learning to accept failure and leverage its lessons transforms it from a loss to a gain.

No one likes to fail. Children are conditioned to avoid it in grade school, and adults almost instinctively try to elude or hide it. Yet, everyone fails, repeatedly in a variety of ways. Failure happens on a spectrum from large, public, and non-recoverable failures like the collapse of a company to small, reversible failures like pilots and experiments. While no changemaker should be cavalier about failures, they should recognize that smaller failures—such as those common to iterative development—are normal and expected.

Iteration means some attempts will work and some will not. Some risks pay off, others don't. Allowing failure leads to bigger and better insights and ideas. It can also prevent more significant failures, saving time, effort, and money. Unfortunately for most, becoming comfortable with failure is on par with eating insects—of conceivable value but sickening to even contemplate.

Minette Norman
Founder Minette Norman Consulting, LLC

When you're leading changes, you're not going to get it all right. You're going to do things that don't work, and then you learn from it, and you go on. I remember one of the mistakes I made when I was changing the localization structure at Autodesk. I had a whole new set of roles, and I decided which roles would be in which of our office locations. And about a week later, someone came up to me and said, "Minette, I think you made a really big mistake. It doesn't make sense to have this role in this location because they have to work with people in a different time zone."

He was right. I think it's important to reward people who will challenge you. I reversed my decision on that, and I was really public about it. I explained that I hadn't thought this through as well as I should, and I got some information later and I credited the person who gave it to me, and I have rethought this, and this is what we're going to do.

You will make mistakes because you're trying to do a lot of stuff at once. You've got a strategy, but you'll get tactics wrong along the way, and those are okay to tweak and revisit if they're not working. I think rigidity is what gets people in trouble, when they're not willing to rethink things. ▲

For many, the prospect of failure cuts a broad swath. It can derail progress, demean efforts, and demoralize teams. It can attack the sense of self, raising doubts about competence, worth, and direction. People fear failure will lower their status, leading to perceptions of them being a loser, inept, and less than others. This isn't only a psychological response. There's evidence that failure provokes biological responses as well, especially in those instances when it's associated with losing a challenge or test. Studies find that the perception of losing lowers testosterone and raises cortisol. Higher cortisol levels make a person more apprehensive, more anxious, and more likely to avoid similar problems or challenges. It decreases resilience, making it more difficult to bounce back.

In professional settings, these reactions are compounded. When failure involves others, such as team members, the feelings can expand to include guilt, shame, and regret. It can dent budgets, drag out timelines, lessen support, and rescope visions. It can lead to layoffs and firings. It can also be the equivalent of chumming the waters for detractors, who are watching and waiting for an opportunity to strike. It can attract people who thrive on the misfortunes of others, bullies who seek opportunities to push people down and gloat over their failures.

In response to failure, most people default to protecting themselves, their position, their behavior, or their team. They may blame a system or context for trapping them or forcing them to make bad decisions. They may point fingers at others, transferring the blame. Or they may even try to hide or ignore it, pretending it didn't happen, or that they had no awareness of it. Alternatively, if they can't find a way to defend against a failure, they might instead take all the responsibility, becoming the "sacrificial lamb" for the team or organization.

A more reasonable stance is to expect some level of failure as a normal part of the changemaking process, as Mexicue founder and CEO, Thomas Kelly, explained:

> *If I was giving advice to someone, I'd acknowledge that there's risk-taking and challenges and fumbles and mistakes. But there's also positives that go with what feels turbulent, chaotic, and negative. It's all part of the territory. If we're going to embrace change, there's going to be some level of failure. You have to communicate that to the team and make that a part of the culture. We're gonna fumble; we're gonna make some mistakes. And that's okay.*

To do this requires creating conditions that permit failure and recognize its value, along with mindsets that accept it and practices that normalize it.

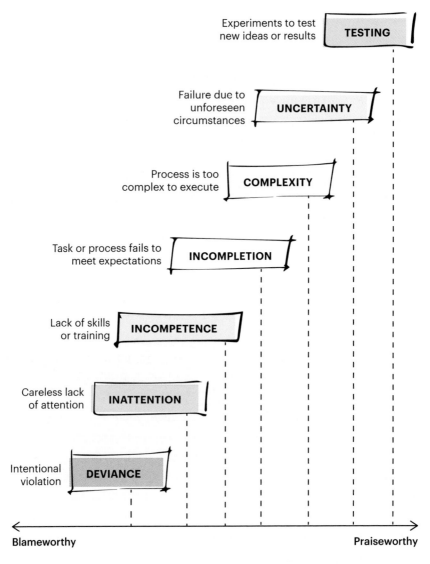

Experiments to test new ideas or results — **TESTING**

Failure due to unforeseen circumstances — **UNCERTAINTY**

Process is too complex to execute — **COMPLEXITY**

Task or process fails to meet expectations — **INCOMPLETION**

Lack of skills or training — **INCOMPETENCE**

Careless lack of attention — **INATTENTION**

Intentional violation — **DEVIANCE**

← Blameworthy   Praiseworthy →

Failure spectrum[1]

1. Failure spectrum is inspired by and adapted from Amy Edmondson's *How Organizations Learn, Innovate, and Compete in the Knowledge Economy.*

Failure as a Coach

An iterative approach to change that accepts failure as part of the process is akin to the approach taken by venture capitalists when they invest in startups. It's impossible for even the most astute and experienced VC firm to predict which startups will succeed, so they fund a range of them. They pay close attention to the markets and other forces influencing their investments, and they encourage pivots or course corrections as needed, accepting that the initial visions are subject to change. Their bet is that most will fail, but one out of a dozen or so will succeed spectacularly well, covering all the other investments. That gamble has been validated countless times over the past several decades.

There aren't many VCs who consider themselves losers. They understand pivots and failure as the costs of success and don't try to judge themselves on any metric that conflicts with that view. Instead, they focus their effort on looking for the best ideas, screening them to determine fit, adding them to the pool, and giving them enough time to explore, alter, rise, or crash. Designers follow an equivalent process when they produce multiple comps or renderings for an assignment. They know that most, and possibly all, will be rejected, but each rejection teaches them what a client likes or doesn't like. It feeds their creative and rational resources and helps them improve the offerings in the next round. In this instance, they don't fear failure. They expect it and use it.

This tactic of expecting failure and integrating it into a regular routine seems unnatural to most people. We see this validated year after year when we assign our students the task of failing. We explain that they should set a goal a bit beyond what they can do or try something new and challenging. We ask them to explain how they failed and how they felt about that experience. Inevitably, we get responses that include feelings of embarrassment, ineptitude, or foolishness. We even get responses explaining that the student failed at failing. But over the years, we've noticed some students who have less trouble with this assignment. Interestingly, most of them are or were serious athletes.

Lessons Learned

Athletes become comfortable with failing because it's their only route to improvement. They can't learn to run faster by reading more textbooks. Writing essays or developing algorithms won't build muscles or refine timing. What leads to improvement is workouts or competitions that push them to the point where they fail—they can't continue because of exhaustion or inability. This helps identify and define where and how they need to improve, whether that's increasing their duration, or acquiring new skills, or adding more practice sessions. Failure becomes a reliable coach: one who sets high goals and pushes performance, but also provides valuable feedback on how to improve.

Changemakers can't all be athletes, but they can emulate their routines using failure as a coach. If an envisioned change project is a "race," then each pilot or prototype is a "heat" that tests performance. A failed experiment merits examination, but not belittlement or quitting. The learning is incorporated, and the team tries again. A simple formula for doing this consistently when experiments don't turn out as planned includes four steps:

Define the failure and accept responsibility. "XYZ has failed. I take responsibility for that." This can be one of the most difficult statements to say out loud, but it's an important starting point in learning from failure. It acknowledges the outcome and initiates the process of defining what happened. That definition may be complex because failure is multifaceted. It can range from dumb to noble. It can be caused by a leader's actions, the actions of others, or circumstances beyond anyone's control. It can be permanent or reversible. Minor or major. The details will vary with each occasion.

In some instances, it helps to start with metrics or hard data that points to what happened. In all instances, the team should hear from those people who experienced the failure. It's not helpful at this point to explain away the failure or try to make it less impactful. The loss needs to be defined as fully as possible, and then the team can move on to the next step of identifying root causes.

Identify root causes. With the points of failure identified and accepted, the next step figures out why it happened. Projects fail for a variety of reasons—some within a team's control and some not. They can fail for a singular reason, for example, because technology didn't perform as it should. Or for multiple reasons, such as people not following instructions, being unclear on what to do, and ignoring feedback. Failure can be the fault of a leader being too driven, as Autodesk's former Chief Product Officer and Co-CEO, Amar Hanspal, admitted:

> *I remember this project that we were trying to pull off, and I was just fed up at one point so I forced action by saying "We're going to build this product, and we're going to ship it on this day!" And I did it with brute force, a lot of the issues unresolved, and people not bought in. The project was a big failure, and I look back and recognize that we got a product out, but it was the wrong product and as a result, it was a missed opportunity. Every time I've done that, something bad has happened. You may feel there's a competitor attacking you or you feel like you're behind in delivering value to a customer, but the hurry-up thing always comes off badly.*

While simple causes may be obvious, like a pilot that was rushed or inadequately supported, digging deeper often reveals reasons that are not as visible. Dispassionate analysis, while difficult to do, is an ideal tool for unpacking these details and determining what went wrong. For example, did the process fail to work as intended, or did the team fail to follow the process? Did the nature of the problem change, or did the team not fully understand the elements of the problem? Zeroing in on the specific points of failure helps to further define the scope and nature of the failure. Is it a complete or partial failure? Is it connected to other developments or standalone? Is it reversible, or not? Giving adequate time and focus to determine the failure's true causes and explore reasons that may be hidden can expand the learning and lead to novel improvements.

Exploring root causes often includes admitting culpability for specific missteps or misjudgments. This admission should be like acknowledging a lost heat or an attempted new dance step—owning the action, not the guilt. A changemaker who owns a failure is better positioned to see what leads to it, and more able to correct it.

Agree on learning. Knowing what went wrong and why it happened usually points to clear learnings. If a process is rushed, the learning is to slow down. If the vision was too grand, the learning is to set more modest goals. These learnings deserve to be fully articulated and shared with the changemaking team and, if relevant, with the broader stakeholder network.

But sometimes the learnings are not clear, or they are disputed. Team members may not see their role in the failure, or they may see it differently than others do. If multiple mistakes led to the failure, there could be disagreement on which mattered more. Even if there's agreement on why the failure happened, there could be multiple perspectives on the corresponding lessons. For example, if the vision was too grand, the learning could be to set goals more modestly, or it could be to procure more resources and a better team.

To conclude this step successfully requires an equal emphasis on portraying the lessons learned clearly and gaining agreement on them. This may take repeated discussion, extended debates, or negotiated agreements, but proceeding without agreement or with muddled learnings can lead to a repeat performance of failure.

Determine what to try next. This step looks at the lessons learned from the failure and decides what to try next. Sometimes, it's a simple adjustment. A widget fails so you fix the widget. But sometimes, it's more challenging. A major failure may be too costly to correct, regardless of how insightful and useful the learning was. It may end the initiative and disband the team. In those cases, the determination of what to do next is a more existential question that can include career repositioning, new responsibilities, or a reexamination of expertise.

A failure may not be significant enough to end the initiative, but still might take time to reinvent or retry. The cause of a failure might be mixed or unknown. In that case, the next attempt isn't guaranteed to work but should at least further uncover the root causes. If a root cause was the resistance of those participating, addressing their issues may need to be prioritized over another attempt. Similarly, if the root cause is traced to a shortcoming among team members, that inadequacy needs to be remedied before moving forward.

Whether simple or more complex, determining what to try next is enhanced by referencing previous positive outcomes. What worked in the past? Could that approach work again in this instance? Does the team have strengths that could be better leveraged in the next round or weaknesses that could be better compensated? Can an expert lend help? Anything that might improve the next outcome is worth considering.

Failure Conditioning

Having a framework to follow in addressing failure helps guide that process, but changemakers also need to build inner strength in dealing with failure. Athletes improve performance through conditioning, and there are similar techniques and exercises that can improve a person's comfort with failure. As with other approaches to growth, it's enlightening to consider biological, psychological, and cultural influences.

The biology of failing is fascinating. If you focus too intently on the failure itself rather than the lessons it offers, your stress levels will remain high. The higher your stress levels, the less your mind can absorb and benefit from the lessons. Given this biological response, an important part of failure conditioning is learning to move beyond the failure and disengage from the stress reflex, to be more open to the learning. This may mean taking time to recover or using other calming techniques that activate the parasympathetic nervous system and trigger the relaxation response in the brain. Or it can mean counterbalancing the feeling of failure by focusing on "wins," as in this example extracted from Christina Wodtke's book, *The Team That Managed Itself*:

> *In the Friday wins session, teams all demo whatever they can. Engineers show bits of code they've got working and designers show mock-ups and maps. Sales can talk about who they've closed, Customer Service can talk about customers they've rescued, Business Development shares deals. This has several benefits. One, you start to feel like you are part of a pretty special winning team. Two, the team starts looking forward to having something to share. They seek wins. And lastly, the company*

starts to appreciate what each discipline is going through and understands what everyone does all day.

Dealing with failure from a psychological perspective can be similar to dealing with death or loss, particularly if expectations were high and the failure was significant. Initially, shock, denial, anger, and other emotional reactions dominate, but upon acceptance and reflection, new meaning emerges and grows stronger over time. With new meaning comes curiosity and creativity, often leading to a renewed purpose and commitment. Sometimes simply recognizing that this is a predictable progression helps calm anxiety and moderate negative self-talk.

A comparable conditioning technique is to gain greater self-awareness around how you think of failure and use this perspective to adjust your mindset. Finding a positive way to react to failure does not mean putting

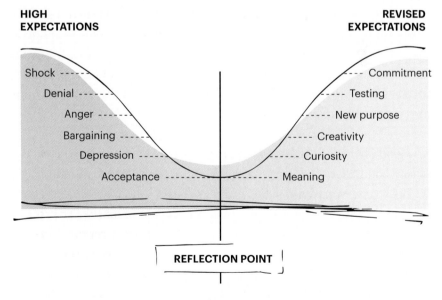

The ups and downs of failure

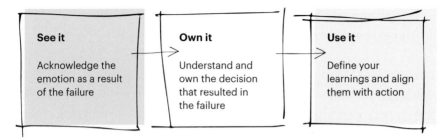

Using failure to change your mindset

a smile on sadness. It means truly seeing the value in the failure and using that value as meaning and motivation. Fortunately, research[2] supports the idea that people can use stress to change their mindsets through a three-step process summarized as "See It, Own It, Use It." It's like the framework for dealing with failure as a team, but more individual in its application.

"Seeing" means acknowledging the stress that failure creates. This acknowledgment moves your thinking from the emotional part of your brain to the rational part, changing your reaction from fear to deliberation. This simple transition puts you in control of your feelings, rather than your feelings controlling you. Your rational brain can focus on planning rather than reacting.

"Owning" the stress means connecting it to its source, understanding the reason you feel it, and welcoming the role it plays for you. Since people typically only stress about those things they value, this step asks why the failure matters to you? In the case of a change initiative, failing may stress you because you doubt your expertise. It may stress you because you feel deeply connected to your team and don't like disappointing

---

2. "Stress Can Be a Good Thing If You Know How to Use It," *Harvard Business Review*, September 2015.

them. Identifying these values clarifies the role that stress is playing and how it's helping you.

The final step, "Use It," takes those values the stress identified for you and helps you align your next actions with them. For example, if your stress at failing was because of the bond you felt with your team, this is a positive attribute. Can you find ways to use your team more strategically or in ways that compensate for shortcomings you have? If your stress at failing was because you doubted your expertise, could you address that through more training, more experience, or maybe a second opinion?

How to Communicate

Sharing failures in a productive and positive manner should earn you a gold medal in communications. Even organizations who claim to value failure often need help living up to that claim. Communications can reinforce the idea that failure is an acceptable part of change by treating it as routine and expected, by embracing those who take risks and suffer failures, and by inviting all to be part of the learning and retrying process.

Deflate failure. You can normalize failure by incorporating it into weekly meetings where everyone is asked to talk about a small misstep or risk they're taking. Attaching a Plan B to any venture implies that failure is a possibility built into all plans. Another way to take the sting out of failure and find more positive aspects in it is to rename it. This may be a psychological trick, but in this case, it works. Words are powerful influences on our thinking, in our communications, and on others' perceptions. Instead of describing it as failure, you can say "setback," or "snag." Instead of failing, you can talk about your "learning a lesson," or "recognizing a new path." Deciding ahead of time to redefine failure in less derogatory terms makes it a strategic move rather than a reaction to criticism.

A related move is to find a positive or optimistic angle to any failure, as Angela Lang, Founder and Executive Director of Black Leaders Organizing for Communities (BLOC), did:

> *Our failures are deeply personal because they're usually tied to our identity in some way, shape, or form. And so to build in added wellness for people to process that shortcoming or that failure, I package it for them. If we lose a candidate we endorsed, part of my job is to find a win in that outcome, and to tell our team that no matter what happens, we're proud of them and the work that they did. Sometimes we don't get the big wins, but let's try to find a small win there, and then pick up the pieces and keep going. And a lot of this is just me as a director trying to make sure I'm adding positivity—which can be very difficult when I just want to crawl into a hole and eat everything.*

Embrace learning. Even if the benefit is positive, it's never easy to deliver bad news. With your team, you'll want to spend more time and go into much greater depth. It may be helpful to do a full deconstruction of the failure—turning it into a story that tells what happened from start to finish. This approach helps team members internalize the lessons and develop empathy for those involved. Rather than a finger-pointing exercise, it focuses on the cause-effect nature of the experiment and failure. This might be best done at an off-site or a similar time when the team can devote more attention to it. Ideally, it should be paired with success stories that can balance out the failures and keep spirits high.

In other stakeholder communications, it's better to be concise. If reporting failure is a part of regular communications, it will raise fewer eyebrows. Depending on the environment, you might humorously title it the "crash and burn" section or seriously label it "lessons learned." Consider asking for input on how best to address the newly discovered problems or what other problems might arise. Providing solutions and giving counsel turns a failure into an opportunity where stakeholders add value. While it can take humility to accept their help, it can be useful to the initiative, and it can increase the likelihood of future success. Whichever approach you take, the explanation should be short and forthright: what went wrong and how you are planning to fix it.

These techniques work with a willing audience, but the challenge increases when dealing with those who can't or won't see the value in failure, or who see it as a means of attacking you and your initiative. In those cases, protection is needed. Avoiding toxic people or people who need too much of your emotional labor to help them feel safe is advisable in all parts of life, but especially in making change. If they can't be avoided, then setting clear boundaries around what is acceptable criticism and what is not can shield you from people whose behavior is abusive.

While it's instructive for leaders to role model how to accept failure, it's not as advisable for them to take the full blame for failures. That position leaves them too vulnerable to others' criticism and sabotage. If risks are prioritized and piloted, and communication is regular and inclusive, failures should be seen as the expected outcome of team-led experimentation. Any explanation of them should avoid singling out individuals and reference the team's role instead.

Takeaways

Failure is part of the process.

Iteration means some attempts will work and some will not. Some risks pay off, while others don't. Everyone involved in the initiative, including stakeholders, needs to understand and support this methodology and its benefits. Allowing failure leads to bigger and better insights and ideas.

No one likes to fail.

Failure attacks the sense of self, raising doubts about competence, worth, and direction. It can lower status, leading to perceptions of being a loser, inept, and less than others.

Let failure be a coach.

To make failure less stressful and more valuable, changemakers learn from it. This approach requires defining the failure, identifying its root causes, agreeing on what's been learned, and determining what to try next.

Recover and try again.

To become personally adept at learning and recovering from failure, changemakers can try biological, psychological, and cultural techniques, including improved self-awareness, renaming of failure, and adoption of practices that "normalize" it.

Take It Further

Being Wrong: Adventures in the Margin of Error.
Kathryn Schulz. Ecco, 2010.

Failing Forward: Turning Mistakes into Stepping Stones for Success.
John C. Maxwell, Henry O. Arnold, et al. Thomas Nelson Inc., 2000.

Overcoming the Dark Side of Leadership: How to Become an Effective Leader by Confronting Potential Failures.
Gary L. McIntosh and Samuel D. Rima. Baker Books, 2007.

The Dip: A Little Book That Teaches You When to Quit (and When to Stick).
Seth Godin. Portfolio, 2007.

The Fearless Organization: Creating Psychological Safety in the Workplace for Learning, Innovation, and Growth.
Amy C. Edmondson. Wiley, 2019.

Chapter 13

When Things Go Right

Success is satisfying. It makes hard work seem more worthwhile, cheers stakeholders and team members, and adds credibility to the initiative and its supporters. For changemaking teams, it's a high-five moment of elation that feeds egos and promotes comradery. It validates assumptions and makes risks seem reasonable. It resupplies energy and ambition, and if it's significant enough, subdues detractors and converts nonbelievers. It's always worthy of note and celebration, provided everyone recognizes it's a brief respite in a long journey.

Like all outcomes, success has its downsides. It may not be as personally rewarding as imagined. It may not bring all the benefits envisioned. It may lead to more work, more challenges, and more stress. In some instances, the changemaker may not be credited with the success. People tend to shrink their role in failure, but with success, their role often grows. The manager who paid no attention to the change initiative may suddenly list it as an accomplishment on his resume. The CEO, who routinely denied requests for more resources, recasts his past behavior as unwavering support.

These moves are unfair but common and rarely worth challenging. From a designer's perspective, every project is a collaboration, with success due to collective effort. Sharing credit broadly, even with those who didn't actually help, may sting briefly, but help generate support for future efforts that may come quickly.

When you are making change, project success is rarely an endpoint or a conclusion. Instead, it's the beginning of careful monitoring and thoughtful scaling to a wider rollout that could continue for several years. Each successful outcome of a pilot or prototype enables the change to scale to a wider audience. In some cases, success immediately initiates another change initiative or introduces a new related goal. In other cases, it's the stimulus that shifts a team's efforts from needing to "push" for change to responding to "pull" for change.

From Push to Pull

Scaling is an incremental, deliberate expansion that ideally leads to a "tipping point"— the point when adoption reaches a critical mass of stakeholders. Tipping points are accelerants. They ensure faster, broader, and deeper acceptance of the change, easing team efforts and signifying more permanent success as Phil Gilbert experienced when he was head of design at IBM:

> *By the end of 2015, through our workshops we had directly reached one-fourth of our product people. These were not the salespeople, not the management, but the designers, the developers, the product managers, and the marketers on the ground. That was when all of a sudden, everybody was using the terms. You had so much cross-pollination from people who had been on teams that were doing design thinking, and now they're on new teams. Even if they hadn't come to our boot camp workshops, they were doing it. Well, that was the tipping point, and it was real. It was really instructional to me.*

From that point forward, we've been very intentional about how we target subsets of the company and then get support from 25% of that part of the business. And we've been very intentional about our communication strategy so that our message and influence spreads.

The concept of a tipping point that accelerates adoption throughout a population was first proposed by Everett Rogers in his classic book, *Diffusion of Innovations*. It was expanded and applied to tech startup scenarios by Geoffrey Moore in *Crossing the Chasm* and made more broadly accessible by Malcolm Gladwell in *The Tipping Point*. The concept is commonly used to track the success of new products or services, but it's rarely considered for internal projects, particularly if an organization pursues top-down change directives or ignores the diverse populations within its ranks. That's a missed opportunity because the diffusion curve's relevance is universal. It can predict the spread of change through an organization from the initial inklings of support to full-spread adoption.

Diffusion

The diffusion curve identifies five subgroups within any population that control the adoption of change. These subgroups—labeled "Innovators," "Early Adopters," "Early Majority," "Late Majority," and "Laggards"— each play a distinct role in accelerating or limiting adoption. Innovators initiate exploration. Early Adopters add credibility. Early Majority add substance and diversity, while Late Majority signal broad acceptance. Laggards may hold out indefinitely or convert only when forced. Understanding the underlying motivations of each subgroup can guide the scaling of a successful pilot.

Innovators have the interest and the patience to try new things, even when they may not work well yet. Their enthusiasm can be an early indicator of potential, but since they tend to be outliers and rarely represent

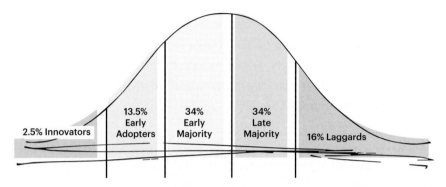

Diffusion of innovation curve

more than 5% of any population, they don't exert enough influence to spur adoption by others. In a change initiative, these people may be willing helpers or stakeholders motivated to work through early bugs and missteps to find a viable solution, but success with them doesn't guarantee anything more.

The first indication of success that could be more widely appreciated will come from a group of early adopters. These stakeholders are more selective about what they are willing to try and more demanding of any outcome. They won't tolerate the problems that Innovators will, but if the change works for them, Early Adopters will promote it to others. This combination of Innovators and Early Adopters, representing about 15–20% of any population, constitutes a "tipping point," where the innovation is likely to spread more rapidly to the rest of the population.

While the diffusion curve is an expedient framework for scaling change, the trajectory doesn't always progress smoothly. Three common traps can slow or stop adoption of change:

The enthusiast dead-end: A piloted experience or a prototype is loved by early innovators but never adopted by anyone else. This is an all-too-common experience of startups who find a small, cohesive group of people who love their product or experience. They focus on those enthusiasts and refine the product for them, assuming they represent a larger group who will eventually come on board. But the product never gains traction beyond this group and the post-mortem reveals that their needs and attitudes were too unique and not reflective of any larger population.

The early adopter "meh": A change explored by innovators moves forward to a broader group of early adopters who also sense merit in it. But when they try it, it fails to excite or satisfy them, and they don't endorse it to any larger group. Instead, they point out its shortcomings—failings that the early enthusiast group didn't mind but that are highly relevant to early adopters.

The large-scale fail: The most significant scaling failure is when all early signs point to success. Innovators love it, early adopters proclaim its value, but when it's adopted by a larger group within the organization, it runs into problems because of some unknown variables or conditions that the pilot experiments didn't catch.

The diffusion model points to many potential hurdles, but it also makes a strong case for incremental scaling. It details why scaling takes time and effort, and it hints at what to monitor and measure with each subgroup. Since most large-scale changes can take at least three to five years to become fully integrated and accepted, this is a valuable reminder and a useful influence.

Monitoring and Measuring

Too many changemakers think of scaling as an end result, not appreciating that each increment of growth leads to the next and that adoption can stall at any time. Careful monitoring and measuring during the rollout and in subsequent months and years can help ensure widespread integration and true success. It does this by providing metrics indicating continued success or possible failure, and also by substantiating the benefits of the change, as Doug Powell attested:

> *We should have been measuring all that we could measure from day one. We just had a blind spot on that, and it took us a couple of years. Now we're pretty good at it, but we missed a couple of key errors. We finally realized that we were coming out of a grace period, and that we needed to talk about the difference we were making. It took us too long to be able to really tell that story effectively.*

To monitor the impact of a change project as it scales is not to police or babysit it. Instead, it's an effective means of determining if changes are being properly implemented and are having the desired effect. Proper monitoring can indicate if a change is stalled and in need of more work, or if it's ready to introduce to a new group. The tricky part is figuring out which aspects of the change to track and measure. Not everything can be monitored, and some aspects of change are more telling than others.

One approach in choosing what to monitor is to assess the level of risk and monitor those aspects of the change that represent the highest risk if they fail. For example, if a company successfully pilots a different way of onboarding new hires, the organization might monitor the rate of new hires who perform satisfactorily at the six-month mark. Or they might track the number of new hires that were successfully onboarded in that time. Or they might monitor the productivity rate of the new hires onboarded under the new approach. The exact aspects monitored will vary from project to project, but they should be consequential and directly related to the primary goals of the change.

A related concern is how long to monitor performance before determining results. Some indicators may be delayed or indirect. For example, if an onboarding process has been changed in order to increase efficiency and job satisfaction, when will that effect be evident? People need time to adjust to new systems. They need time to build new competencies. They might be resistant to reporting satisfaction until they're sure the new system won't backfire.

Regardless of what is monitored and for how long, measurements should be accurate and meaningful. Usually, that means they should be a combination of quantitative and qualitative approaches. Quantitative data, as the name suggests, is numeric. As such, it's usually easier to track, understand, and explain. It tends to be more readily trusted as "truth" and unbiased. It includes KPIs, NPSs, ROIs and other similar measurements—and enjoys widespread acceptance. It can indicate what's happening, often to a precise degree, but rarely can it confirm the reason why something is happening. For example, quantitative data may be perfect for tracking efficiency gains, but will struggle with explaining how efficiency "feels" to people, how it's impacted their life, and whether it's sustainable. It may reveal gains in productivity, but will miss what trade-offs were made. It may highlight wins without noting related, but hidden losses.

Qualitative data typically comes from interviews or observations and tends to be more anecdotal. It can uncover unique insights and reveal emotional reactions, but it's more difficult to confirm and validate. Because of that, it's frequently discounted as unreliable or not representative. However, this type of information can provide the very insights that quantitative data misses. It can explain the mental, emotional, and behavioral impact of any changes made. It can uncover the connections and trade-offs that quantitative tracking can't see.

While the smartest approach to monitoring uses both quantitative and qualitative measures, gathering qualitative input requires more time and labor to ensure its validity and applicability. Stakeholders need to be interviewed, feedback gathered, and regular observations made. An acceptable compromise designs quantitative measures like surveys or streaming data to identify potential problem spots, and then uses qualitative interviews or observations to understand the full nature and cause of those problems. Another approach is to look at trends rather than discrete data points and look for correlations rather than stand-alone indicators. For example, if the onboarding change immediately increases efficiency but not job satisfaction, that's worth exploring further.

An effective monitoring system will identify hits and misses, indicating what's working and what's not. While it's tempting to focus more keenly on fixing what's not working, learning from strengths or successes is just as laudable. Successes indicate where stakeholders are pleased and where they find value in the change. If a change team ignores these sig-

Sam Yen

Head of Innovation, Commercial Banking, JPMorgan Chase

My colleague Janaki Kumar and I noticed that there are four phases of innovation readiness. The first phase is the "lonely soldier phase" where a high-level executive has some sort of "aha" moment about an innovation. The lonely soldier gets assigned to transform the entire organization. They have a small team to do projects, but they're dictated by the executive, and there's a big spotlight on them. If the lonely soldier shows they're able to do things differently with this new methodology and they're creating unexpectedly good outcomes, it's a success.

The second phase is "success in silos," where you start to work on more projects. You've got highly skilled people that were probably part of that initial formation team, and you're starting to get into different parts of the business. You're finding success in silos.

The third phase, which is probably the most critical phase in scaling, is called from "push to pull." Instead of the senior executive (who may not even be in that role anymore), pushing it down, you start seeing other lines of business and other executives start to pull it in. They start contributing, investing, and asking you for help to build out capabilities within their teams.

Then the last phase is "scaled." Scaled is when the organization really starts to transform the people that they hire. They transform the org structures, they transform incentives, they transform processes to really bring this into their organization. ▲

nals, and instead confines their attention to fixing weaknesses, they may miss opportunities for growth. An effective monitoring system will also include some means of determining if change is happening as planned and in line with core principles. If resolving a problem erodes values, it's simply creating more difficulties in the future.

A final detail to consider is who manages the monitoring process. A team member who led the discovery or iteration phase may not be the best person to lead the activities of the scaling phase. This is a phase characterized by routine, precision, and often adept political skills. It requires more planning and deliberation, and less risk-taking and ideation. It deserves someone who enjoys these challenges, but who also appreciates the continuing importance of communication and engagement.

How to Communicate

With successes to report, communication becomes easier and more flexible. Many media options will work in this phase, as long as they have the tendency to spread. You can host workshops with a successfully scaled pilot featured as a case study. You can showcase guest authors who recount specific details of the project. You can record presentations and push the video out to a broader audience, as author Janice Fraser described from her time at Pivotal:

> *When we started at Pivotal in June of 2014, the ratio of developers to designers was 50 to one. Two years later, the ratio was five to one. We accomplished this transformation through workshops and a viral video. I did a lunchtime talk on Balanced Teams. I explained it, and people started sharing. The video was captured, and it got shared around and it was watched, like probably 2,000 times. It's on YouTube right now.*

As change is scaled and rolled out, whatever is being monitored should be reported in the same manner that earlier experiments were communicated: revisions or adjustments noted, metrics translated into language that everyone understands, and improvements categorized as either expected or surprising. How frequently these communications happen depends on the nature of the change and the organization itself. Some may need more regular updates. Others may be comfortable with infrequent updates of notable information. There should be a sense of winding down because that's an accurate reflection of the project's stage, but a complete absence of communication will only restart the rumor mill. Pick a cadence that keeps the initiative alive in the hearts and minds of the organization and provide content that keeps your audience engaged and informed.

This is also a fitting time to remind everyone, through print or in person, of the vision and its impact, to recount the journey and its progress, and to learn from its accomplishments. The framework that helped make failure beneficial in the previous chapter can be repurposed to get the most out of success, providing steps for acknowledging it, identifying and thanking contributors, sharing key learnings, and deciding what comes next.

Acknowledge success and express gratitude. Accepting success and conveying gratitude are positive acts that add momentum to scaling and adoption. But some people have as much difficulty owning success as they do failure. They may fear it's not substantial, the credit is misplaced, or the success will somehow evaporate. They may worry about the consequences of success: that they will be asked to do more or take on greater responsibility. They may not like being in the spotlight, subject to complaints or backlash from others. The mindset exercise introduced to deal with failure works just as well here. Examining why success feels stressful can help identify important values and clarify how to use those values to improve future experiences.

Identify the contributors. Praise others' efforts and make sure that they feel appreciated. Be as specific as possible in pointing out which of their efforts or what expertise led to the success. This makes success more real for people and reinforces that their contributions were seen and mattered. It's unrealistic for everyone to get equal credit—some will have been more instrumental than others, and they should be recognized. But no one should be left out. Even a slight contribution may have had a significant impact. This might even be another opportunity to connect with resistors or detractors to learn why they are not yet on board. Showing them success metrics and inviting them to be part of the next scaling increment could be what finally converts them.

Share learnings. While luck can play a role, success is highly dependent on good judgment and sound decision-making. These learnings can improve others' chances of succeeding, so they should be made widely available. Not in a boasting manner or humble brag ("I'm no genius, but here's how I turned the company around in three weeks"), but rather in a genuine expression of sharing. Making archives accessible, hosting review sessions or "how-to" trainings, and even publicizing the effort and its learnings beyond the organization are generous gifts that can stimulate positive change in other areas.

Decide what's next. This might be a team exercise or a personal one. Perhaps your role now shifts to one of ongoing responsibility for the changes you helped implement. Perhaps the initiative has another phase, or you're ready to lead the same approach in another setting. Or perhaps you want to tackle something completely new. Taking time to think through the next challenge and make decisions about what you want and don't want will prevent you from getting locked into a situation that doesn't suit you.

Takeaways

Success initiates scaling.

When you are making change, success is rarely an endpoint or conclusion. It's the beginning of careful monitoring and thoughtful scaling to a wider rollout.

Find the tipping point.

Scaling is an incremental, deliberate expansion that ideally leads to a "tipping point"—the point when adoption reaches a critical mass of stakeholders. Tipping points are accelerants. They ensure faster, broader, and deeper acceptance of the change, easing team efforts and signifying more permanent success.

Monitor and measure.

Careful monitoring and measuring during the rollout and in subsequent months and years can help ensure widespread integration and true success.

Keep communicating.

How frequently these communications happen depends on the nature of the change and the organization itself. Pick a cadence that keeps the initiative alive in the hearts and minds of the organization. Most importantly, provide content that keeps your audience engaged and informed.

Take It Further

Crossing the Chasm, 3rd Edition: Marketing and Selling Disruptive Products to Mainstream Customers.
Geoffrey A. Moore. Harper Business, 2014.

Diffusion of Innovations.
Everett M. Rogers. Free Press, 2003.

Managing Transitions: Making the Most of Change.
William Bridges and Susan Bridges. Da Capo Lifelong Books, 2009.

Masters of Scale: Surprising Truths from the World's Most Successful Entrepreneurs.
Reid Hoffman. Currency, 2021.

Outliers: The Story of Success.
Malcolm Gladwell. Little, Brown and Company, 2008.

Scale: The Universal Laws of Growth, Innovation, Sustainability, and the Pace of Life, in Organisms, Cities, Economies, and Companies.
Geoffrey West. Penguin Press, 2017.

The Team That Managed Itself: A Story of Leadership.
Christina Wodtke. Cucina Media, 2019.

The Tipping Point: How Little Things Can Make a Big Difference.
Malcolm Gladwell. Little, Brown, 2000.

Chapter 14

Evolving by Design

Projects and initiatives end, but the need for change continues. Solving one problem often generates new ones, and the world will have no shortage of struggles in a future transformed by revolutionary technology, expansive diversity, and the escalating climate crisis. In light of this, Ashoka founder Bill Drayton's description of changemakers is worth considering once again:

> *Changemakers are people who can see the patterns around them, identify the problems in any situation, figure out ways to solve the problem, organize fluid teams, lead collective action, and then continually adapt as situations change.*

Note the last few words explaining that changemakers need to "continually adapt as situations change." This may seem straightforward as a description, but it is not an easy path. It requires constantly scanning the horizon for novel conditions and assessing how to address those new circumstances without sacrificing your values and integrity. It means having the courage to shift direction and the influence to get others to shift with you. It means suffering defeat or disappointment, but not giving up. It also means allowing yourself to adapt, to the future and to the changing nature of your role, your authority, and your challenges.

The early changemakers highlighted at the beginning of this book demonstrate this trait well. José Andrés started World Central Kitchen to provide food relief to disaster zones. He and his organization have continually adapted to new challenges, and have evolved their focus to include training chefs, advocating for nutritional resources, and launching a $1 billion Climate Disaster Fund. José has become increasingly more outspoken and involved in political dialogue. Black Lives Matter continues to advocate for social justice, but has evolved to become more inclusive and more expansive. Web3 entrepreneurs, developers, and community leaders continually face new challenges, iterating at a faster rate than imagined possible as they shift from one course to the next in pursuit of the most viable way forward. Their struggles have no doubt chastened their confidence and deepened their diligence.

Each of these changemakers, and others like them, navigates a continuing series of challenges and hurdles as part of their regular practice. Those experiences hone their ability to stay consistent, believable, and effective in the present, while remaining prepared for future developments that may lead them in a new direction. To do this takes fluidity and the willingness to alter course. It also takes the practical ability to look forward and interpret what may come next, along with the equally useful ability to build and sustain inner strength.

Look Inward

As we've counseled throughout this book, changemakers are not alphas or gurus. They are resilient, persistent pathfinders measured by the coalitions they build and what they set in motion. They are guides and coaches, people who recognize and trust the inherent character and ability of those around them. As such, a changemaker's strength arises out of a defined purpose and passion directed at appropriate problems, in the right environment, and with the right level of support. It's built on an honest acknowledgment of strengths and weaknesses, along with a dependable adherence to personally relevant values. It's fortified by collaboration and comradery.

Those characteristics and behaviors that help changemakers lead transformations need to be updateable and sustainable, as founder of Studio O, Liz Ogbu, ably described:

> *The work that I do is incredibly emotionally taxing. To be able to do it well, I cannot bring my shit back into this situation. I've learned to do that by having a parallel process in which I am doing work on myself, on my ability to handle traumatic situations, and to grieve. As a changemaker, it's not just an external action, it's an internal one, too. You have to create the conditions for change within yourself as much as you do on the outside.*

Appropriate and timely adaption and self-improvement can be nurtured by a disciplined exercise of power, a carefully selected support network, and adequate self-care. These are not luxuries or optional practices. No one questions the self-care of a sports star or celebrity. No one argues that they don't need professional coaching and elaborate support networks to maximize their potential. Those are accepted parts of their jobs that contribute to their performance. That same acceptance should be accorded changemakers.

Power Up

A changemaker's power is determined not only by what a leader has the authority to do, but also by the influence they have and the outcomes they enable. For example, changemakers can have authority over development timelines. They can set deadlines, approve purchases, and discipline team members, but this is not the full extent of their power.

A changemaker's most compelling power may be their ability to calm others, rally crowds, or mediate conflicts.

These powers can and should be elevated and seasoned over time through training, enrichment, and practice. But any overt expression of power needs to be firmly rooted in defined values and integrity and further supported by a web of trusted relationships. There are more than enough examples of people seduced by power who lose sight of who they are and what they stand for. To maintain their dominance, they cater to whatever draws the most attention or greatest rewards to them. They stop being a person with standards and beliefs and instead become an ego that transacts and connives to stay in control.

Strengthening your power without becoming its victim takes discipline. It's shaped and refined by emulating role models you admire and striving to become a role model to others. It's heightened by earning the respect of others, by deserving their trust and confidence. Perhaps ironically, it's fortified by being honest about your weaknesses, as well as your strengths, and by finding the courage to be vulnerable, to say "I'm sorry," and to admit when you're wrong. It's honed by listening to others and carefully considering perspectives different from your own, but also by identifying and calling out self-serving bias in others. It's demonstrated by the ability to say "no," or to leave situations you can't support.

All of these actions are boosted when you speak up for yourself and when you own your identity, as BLOC founder and executive director, Angela Lang, emphasized:

> *I'm an incredibly outspoken person, but it gives me a lot of anxiety, so it's not something I like to do. I remember being really offended by being referred to as an angry black woman because I knew what that trope was. I knew the bias and the stereotypes*

and what a loaded term it was. But then I reclaimed it, and I was like, "Yeah, I am angry because I am a black woman. And that is okay."

Power always has a downside worth monitoring. A potent organizer can tend to micromanage others. A charismatic enthusiast is prone to overschedule herself. A knowledgeable instructor can become preachy. These downsides can be held in check by an effective circle of close associates willing and able to point them out.

Seek Support

Belonging to a community of like-minded individuals is empowering as well as affirming. It can teach and model. It can share and shape. It can unify and protect. Affiliating with a supportive community gives changemakers the opportunity to both give and accept help. A trusted circle of friends and colleagues provides a safe environment where ideas can be tested, complaints aired, and mistakes examined. Finding or building these communities helps changemakers gain from each other, as Stanford lecturer Christina Wodtke explained:

> *One of the things I've done everywhere I go is to find a community I can share knowledge with. If I can't find one, I may start one by saying, "Hey, every Wednesday, let's go get a drink after work and talk about how to manage." That creates a little community. We start talking and having wine or coffee together and discussing what's hard about our jobs, and our strategies on how to navigate it. You cannot navigate intense workplaces by yourself. I've seen this over and over again—if you want resiliency, you need community.*

Support networks are not teams or stakeholder gatherings. They may include individuals from those groups, but their purpose is distinct.

They exist solely to support their members. Because of that, they don't necessarily need to conform to the structural rules of development teams. They may or may not be diverse, and they likely have no hierarchy or defined roles. They are more akin to a circle of friends, albeit with a work emphasis. Finding them can be a serendipitous effort like Christina suggested, or a deliberate selection based on criteria important to the changemaker.

Once formed, a support network does have an obligation to confirm its ethics. Is confidentiality guaranteed? Is transparency promised? Is conflict OK? While these can be sorted out over time, it's less disruptive to clarify them up front. With a shared understanding of what's expected and accepted, a support group can be more relaxed and likely more useful. But support groups can't do all the heavy lifting. For that, you need to accept the responsibility to care for yourself.

Take Care

The risks of changemaking are always high and include existential threats of being fired, discredited, or ignored. Small failures are inevitable, and major ones are possible. Resistance is likely, and more aggressive forms of it—from people who want you to fail—are probable. Priorities are likely to shift, and executive sponsors may be replaced by people who no longer believe in your mission. For highly visible projects, all eyes will be on you, scrutinizing your performance and excusing few missteps. Adding weight to this depressing list is the likely lack of appreciation for a changemaker's role in achieving the desired outcome.

When demands like these exceed the personal and social resources of a changemaker, stress and anxiety levels increase. A mild amount of stress can activate, but chronic stress hampers performance, impairing cognitive, emotional, and perceptual abilities. Stress causes your brain to release hormones like adrenaline and cortisol. In moderation, cortisol is natural and healthy, but when too much is made and accumulated, it can lead to serious illness, as well as reduced sociability, memory, and learning. It can also become addictive, giving rise to changemakers who seek more stress rather than less.

These influences erode a changemaker's ability to lead. With no chance to refuel and reset, burnout sets in, and a burned-out changemaker quickly loses trust and respect. Their decreased capabilities are sensed by others and, if not addressed, they are associated with the change process. Everything comes to a halt or descends into a dysfunctional hodge-podge of uncoordinated efforts, spreading the burnout to others.

Incorporating renewal activities into a daily practice is a potent antidote to the overwork and strain of changemaking, a task author Janice Fraser takes seriously:

> *Changemaking is a marathon. If you're at all successful, it will quickly take over your brain and your life. The people that do this work can have very low points. It feels hopeless sometimes. Even when it's going well, it can be too much. You have to find moments to go to a spa for a week, to let off steam, to have deep close relationships where you can safely rant. This is more personal than most corporate work ever is. And the people who take it on tend to take it on because they believe in something. And when you believe in something, it's possible to let it take over your life. The people I've seen do this well really care very deeply. When you care deeply, you need to have ways to take care of yourself.*

Taking time to restore mental and emotional well-being returns the nervous system to its parasympathetic functioning—a more standard state that is not agitated or stressed. Activities that release oxytocin, such as positive or affirming social situations, counter the effects of cortisol and stimulate feelings of well-being and trust. Offsetting the effects of sustained stress recharges changemakers' energy and enthusiasm, helping them withstand attacks, stay focused on possibilities, and inspire the same in others. It helps them promote and sustain a positive emotional state for all.

For some, this renewal comes from time spent in nonwork environments: family and friends, hobbies or recreational pursuits, avocations or entertainment. For others, it's an intentional mindfulness practice or the escape afforded by vacations or work breaks. The activity matters less than that it is a non-negotiable and regular commitment. The amount of time required for self-care is related to the level of stress. The greater the pressure a changemaker feels, the more self-care he or she needs. This necessity can be ignored or delayed only so long. Stress doesn't fade away; it accumulates until it becomes debilitating. Routine, adequate self-care ensures that day doesn't come.

Look Outward

The combination of sufficient self-care, supportive relationships, and strengthened power improves a changemaker's capability to continually adapt as situations change. It's matched and extended by the ability to look forward and anticipate potential futures.

In a world characterized by volatile, unstable, complex, and ambiguous problems, it's difficult to shift attention from the present to the future, but that's a requirement for changemakers. When you can anticipate the future better, it improves decisions in the present. Focusing ahead provides a buffer, a time to think about options, and the ability to find the best strategy. In short, it provides more flexibility and supports better leadership. The trick is to focus appropriately, as Salesforce Chief Design Officer, Justin Maguire, advised:

> *I like to employ what I call the 15% rule. Imagine a rope tied around your waist back to the company. The length of that rope is about 15%, as in you can be about 15% ahead of the company. If you snap the rope and are out in 20+% land, then you are just viewed as the future person and ignored by those whose job is the here and now. But importantly, if the rope is coiled up at your feet, you aren't doing your job. You need to keep that rope as tight as a guitar string. That is how you help the company move forward. The art in this is assessing what is 15% for your company?*

Determining what is 15% ahead of the present doesn't require a crystal ball or Tarot cards. The view of the future is necessarily fuzzy, but it can be accessed by futures thinking, a defined discipline, complete with experts, institutions, frameworks, and tools, all of which rely on systems thinking and thought experiments common to design and engineering.

Change is supremely important to this discipline. Futurists obsess about change—how it happens, where and when it happens, and how it spreads. They know that change begets more change, but not in a linear fashion. Instead, they recognize that the future unfolds as a complex, dynamic system composed of interdependent elements that make its behavior difficult to model. As a result, they don't try to figure out what the future will be. Just as design encourages multiple solutions, futures thinking encourages multiple futures.

Alternative Outcomes

For most people, the future exists in their minds as a framework of unexamined assumptions about what will happen next. In most cases, these assumptions expect the future to emerge more or less as a straight progression from the present. This view is typically called the "official future." The official future of the United States expects democracy and capitalism to continue more or less unchanged. The official future of business expects profit motives to prevail, and the official future of social infrastructure expects families and friendships to continue forming, food to be easily available, transportation to be affordable, and education to be accessible.

The assumptions that underlie and form official future views are rarely discussed or critically examined, but they should be because they are often wrong, based on untested perspectives, or subject to abrupt revision. As has been amply demonstrated by the impact of the Covid pandemic in 2019, the official future is increasingly wrong. This is happening so frequently of late, that Terry Gilbey put little faith in planning when he was Esalen's CEO:

> *No plan survives engagement with reality. The context changes so quickly today, I think more quickly than it ever has. Outside of a high-level strategic framework, spending time detailing multiyear plans, honestly, I find fruitless these days. We've got massive existential threats, or the black swans, that come at you like floods, fires, pandemics, all of these things. The speed of and the variability in the disruptions is just accelerating.*

Plans or no plans, being able to adapt quickly and agilely is greatly enhanced by having foreknowledge of what's to come. Uncovering and examining the assumptions underlying a simplistic view of the future can produce a more nuanced outlook—one that more accurately captures the multitude of possibilities.

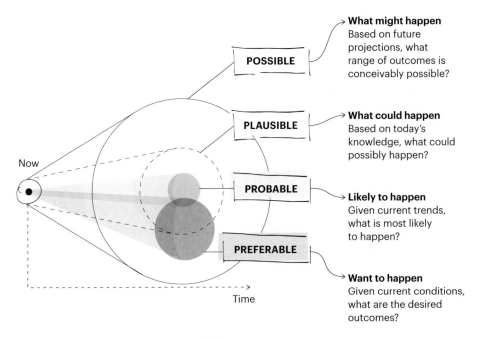

POSSIBLE

What might happen
Based on future projections, what range of outcomes is conceivably possible?

PLAUSIBLE

What could happen
Based on today's knowledge, what could possibly happen?

Now

PROBABLE

Likely to happen
Given current trends, what is most likely to happen?

PREFERABLE

Time

Want to happen
Given current conditions, what are the desired outcomes?

Futures cone

This examination is facilitated by another future thinking tool, the "futures cone." The cone is a model that shows a range of future outcomes, all emanating from the present. The more distant the view, the wider the range becomes, indicating that the accuracy of future projections declines the farther out you look. The range is further defined by the types of futures that can occur. They are categorized as "probable," "plausible," "preferable," and "possible." "Probable" is similar to the official future projection—it's what's most likely to happen if nothing intercedes. "Plausible" indicates a future only slightly different from probable and still largely believable. "Preferable" is a positive spin on the future. This may be a future that's close to the current trajectory or distant from it. Finally, "possible" includes all futures that can conceivably happen, even those that are wildly different from the present.

An organization seeking to modernize their sales process might assume that the future of work will be largely unchanged, with some slight variations for new technology and employee diversity. They might envision that work will continue to be done within companies, will continue to have a profit motive, and that leadership will be human. They might assume a steady supply of employees and clients who value access, service, and reliability. These are all probable outcomes. But alternative assumptions and related trajectories are conceivable. It's possible that computers will take on more significant roles, including leadership. It's plausible that people will want to work for themselves, and that may even be preferable if it is facilitated by government offering a basic income or a more substantial safety net.

Expanded Views

Changemakers who widen their view beyond what is familiar to them improve their view of the future. New assumptions can be surfaced through the review of early signals from social, technical, economic, environmental, or political environments (commonly referred to as STEEP categories). Small modifications to what's considered normal—a new behavior, a new practice, a new policy, a new risk—add up over time to signal bigger alterations on the horizon. They might be evident in emerging trends or predictable progressions like demographics, tech roadmaps, and climate dynamics. Shifts such as declining birth rates, higher education levels, artificial intelligence progress, and rising environmental action are hints of potential futures that changemakers need to recognize and evaluate, not with a traditional lens but with one that considers alternative possibilities.

Finding these breadcrumbs to the future requires paying more attention to those who aren't like you. It involves searching for and learning from different value systems, diverse religious perspectives, alternative governing policies, and the wildly varied goals that motivate and move humanity forward or hold it back. It means being comfortable with science and math, as well as humanities and art. It implies getting out of your comfort zone and creating space for new discoveries.

Tracking and thinking about the implications of different experiences can alert everyone on a changemaking team to the potential of future shifts and can fuel more insightful and productive debates. These influences might suggest more speed or deliberation. They might help weigh one option or another. They might clarify the need for a complete redesign or more modest repositioning. They might help ensure that an envisioned change will work in a future scenario not yet imagined.

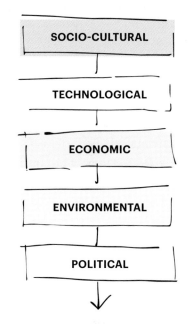

What factors in the future do we need to pay attention to?

How will these factors have an impact on our goals and objectives?

What actions can we take to help mitigate the risk?

Future trend filters

Foreseeing the possibility of alternative futures gives changemakers greater confidence in their present-day actions—not by eliminating ambiguity but by embracing it. They accept the obligation to seek out important and uncertain aspects of the future and try to understand their influences. They know what's next is not linear and predictable, but instead is subject to the influence of competing forces and the erratic nature of human decisions. They use their inner strength—their resilience, power, and flexibility—to adapt to whatever future they encounter and to continue seeing it as a design space.

Design Forward

The future is a function of change, not time. Time passes, but it's change that creates a tomorrow different from today, in minor ways or major, for better or for worse. Any envisioned change arises out of actions taken now.

Changemakers can influence that future as leaders, inspiring others with their vision and capability to make change, encouraging and guiding teams to implement new approaches or systems, and training others to eventually take their place. They can leverage and broaden their influence and impact by helping companies, organizations, and cultures learn to embrace uncertainty and become designers of change themselves. They can do this while retaining a sense of stability and continuity, as Jennifer Deitz, Director and Associate Dean for the Continuing Studies program at Stanford, recommended:

> *If you do change right, there's a freedom and an energy and a synergy that you create with your team or your program by moving with the flow of life, maybe even predicting it a little bit. As exhausting as navigating the Covid pandemic was, it was actually fun and freeing because I had a strong and resilient team that struggled but were ready and interested in figuring out how we could get a professor who's 82 to teach a course on Zoom for the first time.*

The ability that Jennifer cited, "to move with the flow of life," comes from looking outward and inward, continually building inner strength and resilience and applying it to the challenges the future presents. This is more a calling than a job description, and regardless of the size or nature of a changemaker's goals, their actions are admirable and deserving of everyone's attention and respect. These are people who acknowledge problems and challenges, who focus on what matters, and who accept responsibility for finding solutions. They ensure support and build co-creative approaches following a shared process that includes all stakeholders. They communicate the change story in an engaging and honest manner. They define what's possible, envision what can be, iterate, fail, learn, and try again. They persevere and scale what succeeds, and they do this despite the time and the toll it takes.

The world will need more changemakers and more organizations capable of evolving as it struggles with climate change, diversity, technological and medical revolutions, and more. It will need teams that can become more efficient, more interactive, with greater inclusion and compassion. Hopefully, it will continue to recognize the power and potency of design, and to use its special blend of magic to soothe the impact and calm the disruptions of a world where everything is interconnected. A world that can't afford to think and act in provincial ways anymore. A world that can't go backward.

The future will always be imperfect. Even the most accomplished changemaker can't anticipate all that is to come. But perhaps if enough people follow the lead of brave pioneers like José Andrés, the Black Lives Matter collective, and the innovators of Web3, we can return to a time when change is synonymous with improvement. We can become people who figure out how to solve problems, organize fluid teams, lead collective action, and adapt as conditions change. We can live in a world where today's leaders consciously and carefully design tomorrow.

Takeaways

Continually adapt.
Challenges that require the talents of changemakers will continue to surface. To continually adapt as situations change is an essential and ever-present requirement of a changemaker—not only in specific instances, but continually, as a function of who they are and how they react.

Look inward.
Appropriate and timely adaption and self-improvement can be nurtured by a disciplined exercise of power, a carefully selected support network, and adequate self-care.

Look outward.
The ability to work from the present while adapting to possible futures empowers changemakers to gain strength, connect with like-minded communities, and continually sense and adapt as situations change.

Design forward.
Focusing ahead provides a buffer, a time to think about options, and a way to find the best strategy. By foreseeing the possibility of alternative futures, changemakers gain greater confidence in their present-day actions—not by eliminating uncertainty but embracing it. By knowing what's next is not linear and predictable, but rather is subject to competing forces and human decisions.

Take It Further

Comfortable with Uncertainty: 108 Teachings on Cultivating Fearlessness and Compassion.
Pema Chödrön. Shambhala, 2003.

Dare to Lead: Brave Work. Tough Conversations. Whole Hearts.
Brené Brown. Random House, 2018.

How to Relax.
Thich Nhat Hanh. Random, 2013.

Imaginable: How to See the Future Coming and Feel Ready for Anything—Even Things That Seem Impossible Today.
Jane McGonigal. Spiegel & Grau, 2022.

Ten Breaths to Happiness: Touching Life in Its Fullness.
Glen Schneider. Parallax Press, 2013.

The 48 Laws of Power.
Robert Greene. Viking, 1998.

The Art of Resilience: Strategies for an Unbreakable Mind and Body.
Ross Edgley. HarperCollins, 2021.

The Art of Saying NO: How to Stand Your Ground, Reclaim Your Time and Energy, and Refuse to Be Taken for Granted.
Damon Zahariades. Independently published, 2021.

Index

A

accountability
  as responsibility of team members, 94
  in safe environment of co-creation, 77
affiliative decision-makers, 128
Agile process, 84–85, 88
alternative futures, 237–240, 241
analysis, and synthesis, 147–149
Andrés, José, 10–11, 230, 243
Apple, 13, 46
appreciation of others' work. *See* thanking
  others
archives of research findings, 155
Armstrong, Neil, 1
artificial intelligence, as intractable
  problem, 6
Ashoka, 12, 229
assumption mapping, 170
athletes, and failure, 28, 202
audience
  fitting the need, as component of good
    stories, 108–109
  the "who" in communication plan,
    110–111
Autodesk, 105, 128, 145–146, 157, 172–173,
  192–193, 198

B

Barrett, Lisa Feldman, 24
Baxley, Bob, 46
Bethune, Kevin, 81–82, 132–133, 162
bias, 26, 168, 232
Black Leaders Organizing for
  Communities (BLOC), 166, 210

Black Lives Matter, 11, 230, 243
branding a project, 103–105
Bridge Builders, Leapers, and Tradition
  Holders, 123–125
Brooks, Sarah, 59, 90, 127, 154
budget as resource, 60
building support with stakeholders,
  119–137
  alignment with stakeholders,
    119–120
  common ground, finding, 126–127
  connections, making, 120–126
  detractors, dealing with, 128, 130–132
  empathy, 122–123
  goals and incentives, 125–126
  goals and visions, merging, 127–130
  insights, 125
  Leapers, Bridge Builders, and Tradition
    Holders, 123–125
  trust, deepening connections,
    132–135
  visions and values, merging, 127–130
bullies, 199
burnout, 235

C

celebrating wins, 76, 191, 192–193, 215
challengers, as collaboration style, 72
champions for change, 55–58
change
  defined, 21
  designing for, 13–14
  evolution of, and need for, 1–3
  outdated approaches to, 7–10
change fatigue, 46

changemaker, qualities needed in becoming, 21–33
  courage, 23–25
  integrity, 30–31
  optimism, 25–26
  passion, 26–29
  purpose, 22–23
  values, 29–30
changemakers
  adapting to change. *See* evolving by design
  defined, 12, 229
  finding a fit. *See* fit, finding for changemakers
  support networks, 233–234. *See also* building support with stakeholders
changemaking. *See* co-creation of change; envisioning the outcome; failure; foundations of success; learning what works; maps for changemaking; narrative, shaping of; research; success
chapter summaries. *See* takeaways
characters, as component of good stories, 108, 109
climate change, as intractable problem, 6
coaches, as collaboration style, 73
co-creation of change, 65–79
  about leadership, 65–66
  collaboration styles of team members, 71–73
  fluidity of team, 69–77
  group diversity, 66–67
  individual benefits, 67–68
  problems, 67, 68–69
  safe environment for team members, 75–77
  team charter, 73–75
  team strengths and weaknesses, 70–71
collaboration
  in safe environment of co-creation, 76
  styles of leaders, 71–73

collaborative design, 15
communication
  failure sharing, 209–211
  guidelines, as ground rule in operating process, 95–96
  in learning what works, 191–193
  of research findings, 155–157
  strategy, in shaping the narrative, 101–102
  successes to report, 223–225
  of vision, in envisioning the outcome, 175–177
communication options, 102–109
  branding (naming) a project, creating an identity, 103–105
  regular updates, 105–106
  storytelling, 106–109
communication plan details, 110–115
  audience (who), 110–111
  media (how), 113
  purpose (why), 112
  timing (when), 114–115
competence of changemaker, 37–39, 133–134
complex problems
  and design, 14
  as intractable, 5–7
  solving, 181–182
conditioning techniques for failure, 206–209
conflict management, as ground rule in operating process, 97
consequences of making changes, 54
corporate attitudes toward change, 7–10
cortisol hormone, 234–235, 236
costs of making changes, 54, 60
courage, as quality in becoming a changemaker, 23–25
Courage, Catherine, 76, 175
course correcting, in learning what works, 189–190

Covid pandemic
   freedom in moving with flow of life, 242
   and official future, 238
   vaccine as intractable problem, 6
creation, distributed, in envisioning the
   outcome, 165–168
creation of identity, for a project, 103–105
creative brief, 52
creatives, as collaboration style, 72
creativity ("hot streaks"), process leading
   to, 141, 149
crits (critiques), in learning what works, 187
Crossing the Chasm (Moore), 217
cultural flexibility, 45–47

D

DACI (Driver, Approver, Consulted,
   Informed), 93
data, quantitative and qualitative, 221–222.
   See also information from interviews
decision-making
   approaches (rational, affiliative,
      ethical), 128
   data-driven, 42
   in envisioning the outcome, 168–170
   spectrum of, in operating process, 96–97
deep dive, in design research, 147–149
Deitz, Jennifer, 242
delivery, as component of good stories,
   108, 109
demographics, 44
design
   defined, 13
   in modern mindset, 14–16
   from task to strategy, 13–14
design-driven change, 8–10, 17
design principles, in envisioning the
   outcome, 164–165
design processes for change projects, 86.
   See also Double Diamond design
   process

design research. *See* research
designing change, defined, 13–14
designing forward, changemakers
   influencing the future, 242–243
detractors. *See also* resistance to change
   dealing with, 128, 130–132, 146
   and failure, 199
   interviews with, 146
   in road shows, 156–157
diffusion curve, 217–219
Diffusion of Innovations (Rogers), 217
directive, as pillar for foundation of
   success, 52–54
directors, as collaboration style, 71–72
disaster relief kitchen, 10–11, 230
Disneyland, change and progress, 2, 7, 17
distributed creation, in envisioning the
   outcome, 165–168
divergence-convergence model, 86
diversity
   in co-creation teams, 66–67
   in sensemaking phase of research, 150
DNA, decoding of, 6
domain knowledge, 38
Double Diamond design process, 86–88
   define stage, 86, 89
   deliver stage, 87, 89
   develop stage, 86–87, 89
   discover stage, 86, 88
   modified for making change, 88–90
Drayton, Bill, 12, 229

E

early adopters, on diffusion curve, 217–219
early majority, on diffusion curve, 217–218
Edmondson, Amy, 200
empathy, in building support, 122–123
engagement, executive, 44
engineering problems in construction, 6
enthusiast dead-end, 218–219

environment
the right one for a changemaker, 41–47
safe, for team members, 75–77
envisioning the outcome, 161–162
approach to, 161–162
decisions, 168–170
design principles, 164–165
distributed creation, 165–168
priorities, projects, and plans, 171–175
process of, 164
vision, communication of, 175–177
vision, creation of, 163–164
Esalen Institute, 27, 238
ethically-oriented decision-makers, 128
evolving by design, 229–245
alternative futures, 237–240
changemakers adapting to change,
229–230
changemakers' characteristics, 230–231
changemakers designing the future,
242–243
changemaker's power, 231–233
expanded views, 240–241
looking to future, 236–237
stress and self-care, 234–236
support networks, 233–234
executive engagement, 44
expectations, of directive and sponsor,
57–58
Expedia, 125
experimentation. *See* learning what works
expert panels, 188

F

Facebook, designing change, 13
failure, 197–213
about, 197–199
biological and psychological responses,
198, 206–207
as a coach, 201–209
communicating, 209–211
deflating with words, 209–210

failure conditioning, 206–209
failure spectrum, 200
learning from failure, 202–205, 210–211
faking it, 36
Farther, Faster, and Far Less Drama
(Fraser), 74–75
fear, xi, 25
feedback, in learning what works, 187–189
fight, flight, or freeze, 24–25
fill-ins, in Impact Matrix, 173–174
finance approach to change, 7
fit, finding for changemakers, 35–49
alignment, 35–36
competence and strengths, 37–39
cultural flexibility, 45–47
leveling up, 39–40
openness to change, 42–45
right environment, 41–47
right problem, 36–40
flexibility, 93
fluidity in co-creation of change, 69–77
foundations of success, 51–63
about pillars of support, 51–52
champion or sponsor, 55–58
clear directive, 52–54
realistic expectations, 57–58
sufficient resources, 58–61
fragmented world, 3–5
Fraser, Janice, 74–75, 223, 235
from push to pull, innovation phase, 222
future, imperfect, 1–19
about change, 1–3
designing change, 13–14
fragmented world, 3–5
future of change, 10–16
impediments to change and progress,
3–10
intractable problems, 5–7
modern mindset, 14–16
outdated approaches to change, 7–10
reason for this book, 16–17

future, the official, 238–239
futures, alternative, 237–240, 241
futures cone, 239
futures thinking, 237
futurists, 237

G

gamifying feedback, 188
Gartner Hype Cycle, 189
Gilbert, Phil, 38, 56, 103–104, 216–217
Gilbey, Terry, 27, 238
GitHub, 172
Giudice, Maria, 145–146, 157
"give and take" between stakeholders
    and changemakers, 129
Gladwell, Malcolm, 217
goals and incentives in building support,
    125–126
Google, designing change, 13
gratitude. *See* thanking others
grit, 27–28
ground rules
    in getting feedback, 188
    in operating process, 94–97
growth, in structural openness,
    43–44

H

Hanspal, Amar, 128, 173–174, 192, 203
"Happy Hour" on Fridays, 193
Heraclitus, xi
Hoffer, Dave, 39–40, 121–122, 129,
    185–186
Holmes, Kat, x–xi
*How Organizations Learn, Innovate and
    Compete in the Knowledge Economy*
    (Edmondson), 200
human-focused, design as, 15

I

IBM
    designing change, 13
    executive sponsorship at, 56
    naming projects, 103–104
    stating vision as one word, 176
    tipping point, 216–217
ideation sessions, 167
Impact Matrix, 173–174
imperfect future. *See* future, imperfect
information from interviews, self-reported
    and extracted, 146–147. *See also* data
innovation
    phases of readiness, 222
    as technology-driven change, 8
innovators, on diffusion curve, 217–218
integrity
    as component of trust, 133–135
    as quality in becoming a changemaker,
        30–31
intention, as component of trust, 133–134
interviews of stakeholders, 142–147
intractable problems, 5–7
Ireland, Christopher, 193
iteration, in implementation of change, 171
iterative development, 182–186
    failure in, 197, 202
    pilots and pivots, 183–185
    prototyping to make it real, 185–186

J

Jobs, Steve, 28, 65, 181
journey maps, in sensemaking phase of
    research, 150–152, 153–154
JPMorgan Chase, 140, 156, 222

K

Kelly, Thomas, 28, 44–45, 199
key results, 91–92
King, Martin Luther, 65

KPIs (Key Performance Indicators), 91
Kumar, Janaki, 140, 222

L

laggards, on diffusion curve, 217–218
Lang, Angela, 166–167, 210, 232–233
late majority, on diffusion curve, 217–218
leadership, in co-creating change,
    65–66, 69
Lean Startup operating process, 85, 88
Leapers, Bridge Builders, and Tradition
    Holders, 123–125
learning from failure, 204–205, 210–211
learning what works, 181–195
    communicating, 191–193
    complex problems, solving, 181–182
    course correcting, 189–190
    crits (critiques), 187
    feedback, getting, 187–189
    iterative development, 182–186
    pilots, 183–185
    prototyping to make it real, 185–186
learnings from success, sharing, 225
leveling up, 39–40
listening tour, 145–146
lonely soldier, innovation phase, 222

M

Maguire, Justin, 77, 110, 143, 237
major projects, in Impact Matrix, 173–174
manufacturing approach to change, 7
maps for changemaking, 81–99
    about the right process, 81–82
    choosing the right process, 82–90.
        See also process options in
        changemaking operations
    rules of engagement, 90–97. See
        also rules of engagement, for
        changemaking process
market fit, 35

McDonald, Bob, 59
measuring, for success, 219–222
media, the "how" in communication
    plan, 113
mindset
    modern, 14–16
    using failure (or success) to change,
        208–209, 224
minimum viable product (MVP), 186
models, in sensemaking phase of research,
    150–152
monitoring and measuring, for success,
    219–223
Moore, Geoffrey, 217

N

naming
    a project, 103–105
    renaming failure, 209–210
narrative, in sensemaking phase of
    research, 154
narrative, shaping of, 101–117
    about communication strategy, 101–102
    communication options, 102–109. See
        also communication options
    details of communication plan (who,
        why, how, when), 110–115
NeuroLeadership Institute, 130
Norman, Minette, 105–106, 172–173, 198

O

Obama, Barack, 28, 59
objectives of project, 91–93
observations, 142
official future, 238–239
Ogbu, Liz, 30, 107, 231
OKRs (Objectives and Key Results), 91
openness to change, 42–45
optimism, as quality in becoming a
    changemaker, 25–26

optimistic bias, 26

organizational structure, 42

outdated approaches to change, 7–10

P

participation, enticement of, in learning what works, 192–193

participation standards, as ground rule in operating process, 94–95

partnering, in co-creation of change, 70

passion, as quality in becoming a changemaker, 26–29

personas, in sensemaking phase of research, 150–152, 153

personnel as resource, 60–61

photos, as communication in learning what works, 191–192

pilots and pivots
in iterative development, 183–185
showcase pilots, 191–192

Pinterest, culture and values, 46

Pivotal, 223

plans
in envisioning the outcome, 174–175
and the official future, 238
project objectives and, 91–93

Powell, Doug, 56, 125, 176, 220

power of changemakers, 231–233

praise for others. *See* thanking others

Presidential Innovation Fellowship, 59

"pretend VC," 188

priorities, in envisioning the outcome, 171–175

problem (or opportunity)
the right one for a changemaker, 36–40
summarizing in sensemaking phase of research, 153

problems
intractable, untamed, wicked, 5–7
solving complex problems, 14, 181–182

VUCA (volatile, uncertain, complex, and ambiguous), 5

process options in changemaking operations, 82–90
Agile process, 84–85
design processes, 86
Double Diamond model, 86–88
Double Diamond modified for changemaking, 88–90
Lean Startup, 85
Waterfall, 83

progress check-ins, as ground rule in operating process, 94

project managers, as collaboration style, 72

project objectives and plans, 91–93

projects, in envisioning the outcome, 171–175

prototyping, in iterative development, 185–186

purpose
as quality in becoming a changemaker, 22–23
the "why" in communication plan, 112

push to pull, innovation phase, 222

Q

qualitative data, 221–222

quantitative data, 221–222

R

RACI (Responsible, Accountable, Consulted, Informed), 93

recognition of effort. *See* thanking others

red team/blue team exercise, 188

re-engineering, 7

rehearsal in storytelling, 109

research, 139–159
approach for creativity bursts, 141
communication of research findings, 155–157

deep dive with analysis and synthesis,
147–149
framework to identify options,
152–154
informing and inspiration, 139–140
listening tour, 145–146
models and visualizations, 150–152
scans, observations, and interviews,
142–147
sensemaking, 149–154
stakeholder types, in interviews,
143–144
wide view phase, 142–147
resilience, 28
resistence to change. *See also* detractors
finding during course correction, 190
reasons for, 41, 122–123
SCARF model, 130–131
sources of, 54
resources
budget as, 60
personnel as, 60–61
in structural openness, 43
sufficient for success, 58–61
time as, 59–60
written. *See* take it further
responsibilities
for failures, 202–203
for team members in operating process,
93–94
risks
defined in team charter, 74–75
in envisioning the outcome, 169–170
road shows, 156–157
Rock, David, 130
Rogers, Everett, 217
roles
finding the right fit, 39–40
for team members in operating process,
93–94
Ross, Ivy, 149

rules of engagement, for changemaking
process, 90–97
communication guidelines, 95–96
conflict management, 97
decision-making, 96–97
ground rules, 94–97
participation standards, 94–95
plans, 91–93
progress check-ins, 94
project objectives, 91–92
roles and responsibilities, 93–94
shared agreements, 90–91
timelines, 91–93
tool choice, 95

S

Salesforce, 77
scaled, innovation phase, 222
scaling, 216, 219–220
scans, 142
SCARF model, 130–131
Schleuning, Amber, 59
second-order thinking, 170
"See It, Own It, Use It," 208–209
self-care for changemakers, 234–236
sensemaking phase of design research,
149–154
shared agreements, for operational
process, 90–91
shared values, in team charter, 73–74
Sharot, Tali, 26
showcase pilots, 191–192
Silicon Valley, 16
smallpox, 6
social attitudes toward change, 7–10
social entrepreneur movement,
defined, 12
solutions, offering in sensemaking phase
of research, 154
sponsors for change, 55–58

sprints, 141

stakeholder map, 144–145

stakeholders. *See also* building support with stakeholders
    interviewing, 142–147
    testimonials, 156
    types of, 143–145

startups
    culture of, 7–8, 10
    Lean Startup operating process, 85, 88
    Leaper mentality, 123
    structural and cultural openness at, 47

STEEP (social, technical, economic, environmental, and political) future trend filters, 240–241

storyboards
    in communication of vision, 177
    in sensemaking phase of research, 151–152

storytelling, 106–109. *See also* narrative, shaping of
    benefits of, 106–108
    components of good stories, 108–109

strategies, traditional, 161

strengths
    of changemaker, 37–39, 230–231
    of team members, 70–71, 93–94

stress in changemakers, 234–236

structural openness, 42–45

success, 215–227. *See also* foundations of success
    about, 215–216
    communication, 223–225
    diffusion curve, 217–219
    monitoring and measuring, 219–223
    reasonable and unreasonable definitions of, 57–58
    tipping points, 216–217, 218

success in silos, innovation phase, 222

summaries of chapters. *See* takeaways

support. *See* building support with stakeholders

support networks for changemakers, 233–234

swimming upstream, 41, 55

synthesis, and analysis, 147–149

T

take it further (written resources)
    building support with stakeholders, 137
    co-creation of change, 79
    envisioning the outcome, 179
    evolving by design, 245
    failure, 213
    finding a fit for changemaker, 49
    foundations of success, 63
    imperfect future, 19
    learning what works, 195
    maps for changemaking, 99
    qualities in becoming a changemaker, 33
    research, 159
    shaping the narrative, 117
    success, 227

takeaways (chapter summaries)
    building support with stakeholders, 136
    co-creation of change, 78
    envisioning the outcome, 178
    evolving by design, 244
    failure, 212
    finding a fit for changemaker, 48
    foundations of success, 62
    imperfect future, 18
    learning what works, 194
    maps for changemaking, 98
    qualities in becoming a changemaker, 32
    research, 158
    shaping the narrative, 116
    success, 226

team charters, 73–75

team players, as collaboration style, 72

The Team That Managed Itself (Wodtke), 206

teams, in co-creation. *See* co-creation of change

technology-driven change, innovation as, 8

testing what works. *See* learning what works

thanking others
  appreciation of others' work, 74, 75, 102, 103, 122, 129, 225
  expressing gratitude, 129, 165, 224
  praise for others, 173, 186, 200, 225
  recognition of effort, 73, 74, 76, 119, 165

thankless tasks, in Impact Matrix, 173–174

time as resource, 59–60

timelines, in operating process, 91–93

timing, the "when" in communication plan, 114–115

The Tipping Point (Gladwell), 217

tipping points, 216–217, 218

tool choice, as ground rule in operating process, 95

Tradition Holders, Leapers, and Bridge Builders, 123–125

tribalism, 5

trust
  in building support and connections, 132–135
  components of, 134

U

untamed problems, 5

updates, and regular communication, 105–106

V

V.A. Center for Innovation, 59

values
  merging with supporters, 127
  as quality in becoming a changemaker, 29–30
  shared, in team charter, 73–74

venture capitalists
  "pretend VC" game, 188
  view of pivots and failure, 201

veterans, project for, 59

vision
  communication of, 175–177
  creation of, 163–164
  merging with supporters, 127–130

visualizations
  communicating in learning what works, 191–192
  in sensemaking phase of research, 150–152

VUCA (volatile, uncertain, complex, and ambiguous) problems, 5

W

"war room," 155

Waterfall operating process, 83

weaknesses
  of changemaker, 39, 231
  of team members, 70–71

Web3, 11, 184–185, 203, 243

wicked problems, 5–7

wide view, in design research, 142–147
  interviews, 142–144
  observations, 142
  scans, 142

wins
  celebrating, 76, 191, 192–193, 215
  small and quick, 172–174

Wodtke, Christina, 68, 184, 206, 233

words
  in communication of vision, 176
  deflating failure, 209–210

World Central Kitchen, 11, 230

Y

Yahoo, 68

Yen, Sam, 156, 222

Acknowledgments

In addition to the contributors acknowledged in the opening pages of this book, several other people deserve our thanks. We are grateful for their support, collaborative nature, and notable creativity:

First and foremost, we'd like to thank Lou Rosenfeld, our publisher, and Marta Justak, our managing editor, for trusting our vision and giving us the latitude and flexibility needed to create the book we wanted to see in the world.

We are deeply grateful to our amazing design team. Christopher Simmons from MINE set the book's tone through his thoughtful and provocative interior design. Aino Horsma created beautiful, artistic illustrations and graphics throughout the book, elevating it to the next level of "awesomeness." David Van Ness produced the book with good humor and grace, along with incredible attention to detail. Jason Kernevich from Heads of State visually captured the book's content in his fresh cover illustration. John Cantwell lent his intelligent wordsmithing to the subtitle of the book and related marketing support.

Special thanks to Kat Holmes for writing such a brilliant foreword and to all those who wrote heartfelt testimonials in support of our book.

We are so indebted to our generous friends and family members who reviewed early, almost unreadable, versions of this book and provided invaluable feedback: MacKenzie Masten, Kelley Ireland Kelly, Joe Herold, Kerry Ireland, Brenda Laurel, Nancy Deyo, and Kristee Rosendahl.

We appreciate the many clients and colleagues who enabled us to learn in real time and develop the skills necessary to navigate the messy processes and people dynamics inherent in designing change at scale. We are paying their trust in us forward by helping others follow in our footsteps.

To our families and friends who patiently waited for us to stop obsessing over every element of this book, to restack the dozens of books we reviewed, and to close our computers and rejoin them at the dinner table, we know our thanks are not enough. We promise to be more present in the next year.

Maria would especially like to thank her husband, Scott Allen, and her two children, Maxwell and Olivia Allen, whose love, support, and great patience provided the solid grounding for Maria to work, along with added wit, sarcasm, and humor. Maria would also like to thank her sister, Terri Giudice-Lewis, because she is the best sister in the world.

This book is the byproduct of not only Maria and Christopher's shared experiences, but also their deep love and respect for each other. We are incredibly grateful that the universe had the good sense to bring us together.

About the Authors

Maria Giudice

Throughout her illustrious career, creative teams and business leaders have sought the provocative vision and mentorship of Maria Giudice. As founder and CEO of the pioneering experience design firm Hot Studio, Maria built a thriving practice around the principles of human-centered design. Today, former "Hotties" can be found leading teams at Adobe, Google, McKinsey, Airbnb, Pinterest, Twitter, Meta, and more.

After Hot Studio's acquisition by Facebook in 2013, Maria led global design teams at Facebook and Autodesk, building digital experiences for millions worldwide. And now, after three decades at the forefront of business and design, Maria has a new mission—building the next generation of creative leaders. Through one-on-one coaching, group coaching, and team-building workshops, Maria unlocks the potential hidden in executives and the people they lead.

A popular speaker at design and business conferences, Maria is the co-author of several design books, including *Rise of the DEO: Leadership by Design*, which has been translated into several languages. Maria teaches design leadership at Stanford Continuing Studies and California College of the Arts, where she is also a trustee. Maria is a member of several advisory boards.

Christopher Ireland

Researcher, strategist, idea generator, and alliance builder—Christopher Ireland started her career with the notion that businesses could benefit from a better understanding of people and culture. Her ability to create simple explanations of complex human behavior and to translate those insights into effective design and development strategies attracted clients from both technology and consumer goods companies, including Microsoft, Apple, Pepsi, Levi's, GM, and more.

As co-founder and CEO of Cheskin, a firm that pioneered design research in Silicon Valley, Christopher and her partners had ringside seats to unrivaled feats of creation, innovation, and reinvention. Beginning in the 1990s, she led teams exploring topics like how trends move through the teen population, how music relates to mood, the history of residential architectural styles, the power of play, the cultural and behavioral differences of girls and boys, the emerging culture of "cool" in China, the development of trust online, and the meaning of color around the globe—to name just a few. She and her partners sold Cheskin in 2007 and walked away with their sanity mostly intact.

Christopher is a co-author of *Rise of the DEO: Leadership by Design* and *China's New Culture of Cool*. She received an MBA from UCLA and currently teaches leadership and design strategy courses for Stanford University's Continuing Studies Program.